Metatron

Connecting with the Archangel of Empowerment

© Copyright 2024 – All rights reserved.

The content contained within this book may not be reproduced, duplicated, or transmitted without direct written permission from the author or the publisher.

Under no circumstances will any blame or legal responsibility be held against the publisher, or author, for any damages, reparation, or monetary loss due to the information contained within this book, either directly or indirectly.

Legal Notice:

This book is copyright protected. It is only for personal use. You cannot amend, distribute, sell, use, quote or paraphrase any part of the content within this book, without the consent of the author or publisher.

Disclaimer Notice:

Please note the information contained within this document is for educational and entertainment purposes only. All effort has been executed to present accurate, up-to-date, reliable, and complete information. No warranties of any kind are declared or implied. Readers acknowledge that the author is not engaging in the rendering of legal, financial, medical, or professional advice. The content within this book has been derived from various sources. Please consult a licensed professional before attempting any techniques outlined in this book.

By reading this document, the reader agrees that under no circumstances is the author responsible for any losses, direct or indirect, that are incurred as a result of the use of the information contained within this document, including, but not limited to, errors, omissions, or inaccuracies.

Your Free Gift
(only available for a limited time)

Thanks for getting this book! If you want to learn more about various spirituality topics, then join Mari Silva's community and get a free guided meditation MP3 for awakening your third eye. This guided meditation mp3 is designed to open and strengthen ones third eye so you can experience a higher state of consciousness. Simply visit the link below the image to get started.

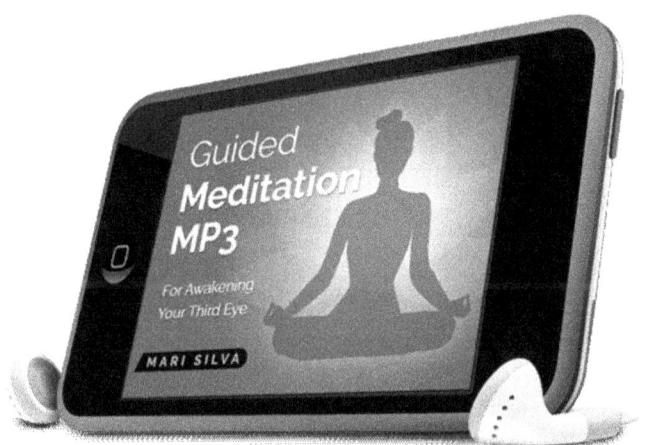

https://spiritualityspot.com/meditation

Table of Contents

INTRODUCTION 1
CHAPTER 1: WHO IS ARCHANGEL METATRON? 3
CHAPTER 2: ASCENSION WITH METATRON 14
CHAPTER 3: RECOGNIZING METATRON'S PRESENCE 25
CHAPTER 4: METATRON'S CUBE 35
CHAPTER 5: PILLAR OF LIGHT MEDITATION 46
CHAPTER 6: ANGELIC REIKI AND HEALING 56
CHAPTER 7: CRYSTALS TO CONNECT WITH METATRON 68
CHAPTER 8: CORD CUTTING AND SHIELDING 81
CHAPTER 9: DAILY MEDITATIONS 91
BONUS: CORRESPONDENCES SHEET 101
CONCLUSION 110
HERE'S ANOTHER BOOK BY MARI SILVA THAT YOU MIGHT LIKE 112
YOUR FREE GIFT (ONLY AVAILABLE FOR A LIMITED TIME) 113
REFERENCES 114

Introduction

Angels are all around you. They are guiding you, protecting you, and watching over you. Everyone wants to know they aren't alone and that someone out there is watching over them. The idea that these higher beings exist can make you feel safe, and no matter how hard life can get, thinking of angels can provide solace in dark times.

Although millions of angels exist in the world, you can find yourself drawn to just one. Perhaps they heard your prayers and want to help you, or they want to reach out to you to guide you or warn you against danger.

Metatron is one of the most significant angels few people are familiar with, but he is a powerful being who can be very supportive and beneficial to have by your side.

This book begins by introducing the angel Metatron and his origin. It then explains the angelic kingdom so you can better understand his role in their hierarchy. Metatron is also mentioned in many mystical texts, which the book will cover in detail. You will also discover his various attributes and epithets and what they mean. The book will also highlight his different aspects and connection with Enoch.

You may be familiar with the concept of ascension, but do you know what it means? Or how can you achieve it through connecting with Metatron? The book will answer these questions and explain the benefits of this process and how you can recognize when it is happening.

When you reach out to Metatron, he will try to connect with you. However, he won't do this directly. Each angel has their own signs they send to humans to announce their presence. The book will discuss these symbols and recount the personal experiences of some people who managed to connect with the angel.

The following chapter introduces and explains Metatron's Cube and its connection with sacred geometry. The book will then return to the concept of ascension by introducing the Pillar of Light exercise. It will also discuss meditation, its origin, and how to use it to receive Metatron's energy.

The book continues to introduce and explain the concept of Reiki and its origins. You will also learn about angelic Reiki, its principles, and how to use it to develop a deeper connection with Metatron. You will then learn about crystals and how they can heal your body and spirit. Since there are many types of stones, the book will introduce the most common ones, their properties, and which ones work with Metatron.

The last part of the book will focus on cord-cutting and energetic shielding when Metatron is present. It will explain both concepts, their benefits, and how to practice them. Finally, you will learn daily exercises and techniques to strengthen your connection with Metatron.

This book will introduce you to the world of Metatron and provide tips, techniques, and exercises with step-by-step instructions to connect with him. All the information is presented in simple language so beginners can easily understand it.

Transform your life, and let Metatron empower and heal you.

Chapter 1: Who Is Archangel Metatron?

Metatron is often described as one of the most enigmatic Archangels inhabiting the heavenly realm. He is highly praised by Hebrew mythology, yet his origins are shrouded in obscurity. Present in Christian and Jewish mystical traditions, the roles of Metatron have always fascinated those who came across them in their studies or spiritual practices. Besides being seen as the highest-ranking Archangel in Hebrew mythology, Metatron is mostly known as the angel of empowerment. He can help further spiritual elevation and achieve a level of growth that ultimately leads to the ascension of the spirit.

This first chapter introduces this angelic archetype, including the etymology of his name and the origins of the figure. Reading it, you learn about the angelic hierarchy and Metatron's role. You'll also get the opportunity to explore Metatron's different attributes and epithets as viewed by the range of cultures and belief systems in which he appears. Lastly, you'll learn about the long-standing debate of whether Archangel Metatron can be equated with another powerful Archangel, Michael.

The Angelic Kingdom and Hierarchy

The angelic hierarchy.
Andrewrabbott, CC BY-SA 4.0 <https://creativecommons.org/licenses/by-sa/4.0>, via Wikimedia Commons: https://commons.wikimedia.org/wiki/File:West_window,_St_Michael_and_All_Angels%27_Church,_Somerton.jpg

To understand better who Metatron is, it's necessary to first explore the angelic kingdom as a whole. According to Islam, Christianity, and Judaism, the celestial kingdom has a complex hierarchy system determined by three energetic spheres. The spheres divide the hierarchy into nine different orders and ranks – starting with the beings closest to the divine and ending with the angels closest to people. The hierarchy helps establish and maintain the divine order and balance all creations that need to exist.

The origins of the divine hierarchy concepts are attributed to Pseudo-Dionysius the Areopagite, a 5th-century theologian who spent a copious amount of time studying and deciphering the roles of divine beings. Based on the hierarchy established by Pseudo-Dionysius, the angelic beings are ranked into a clear and beautiful system described below. Each angelic structure highlights the diverse positions and obligations angels play in the celestial kingdom.

Sphere I

This sphere includes the beings closest to the ultimate divine essence – the Thrones, the Cherubim, and Seraphim.

As their name implies (the word "seraph" is translated as "the burning one"), Seraphim are the angels burning with the highest power of the divine. According to some sources, the prophet Isaiah (who visited the celestial realm) described Serahim as tall beings with six wings. Their entire body is covered in light. They use one pair of wings for flying, one to shield their eyes, and one pair to cover their feet. Their roles include honoring and praising the Divine and caring for spiritual nourishment.

The Cherubim are celestial protectors with many faces, including that of an eagle, an ox, a lion, and a man). They have four wings covered with eyes and body parts resembling animal parts. For example, their feet look like the cloven hooves of an ox, while their body is as powerful as a lion's. They are also the guardians of the Garden of Eden and were first described by Ezekiel, who believed that the fallen angels once belonged to the ranks of Cherubim.

The Thrones take care of the celestial throne, thus, are tightly linked to its authority and judicial power. They are responsible for establishing justice in the angelic realm. Besides being the patrons of divine justice, the Thrones are also connected to the Ophanims – also known as *Wheels* in Jewish celestial mythology. In Daniel's visions, the Thrones appear as strange creatures resembling unique wheels that also have other wheels in them.

Sphere II

The second sphere belongs to the governors of all beings. The Dominions, the rulers of the angelic world, occupy the first order. They assign and oversee the duties of all angels, who call them lords (or lordships). They have a humanlike appearance, except for their prominent wings, often depicted shining bright with divine light. The Dominions can be distinguished from other angels by the orb of light shining on top of their swords and scepters.

This sphere also includes the Virtues, the angels who bring miracles. Due to this, they're considered the most influential angelic beings. They help people manifest miracles by providing divine strength. Some of the miracles they manifest include foretelling the future, healing illnesses, and guiding people toward their life's purpose. The Virtues are the first angelic order in direct communication with people. By bestowing them the gift of patience, resilience, humility, and courage, the Virtues assist people in spiritual growth and accepting the power of divine love.

Lastly, there are Powers, the angelic warriors responsible for dispelling evil influences. They fight off malicious spirits threatening the celestial realm and supervise the interactions of celestial beings with all spirits. This way, they maintain the balance and security of all beings in the celestial kingdom. The powers are portrayed as magnificent creatures equipped with weapons, armor, shields, and helmets – a true picture of a heavenly army.

Sphere III

The third sphere of the celestial kingdom is reserved for the Principalities, Archangels, and all the other Angels. The Principalities are closely connected to people; they are the patrons of nations, ethnicities, and institutions. They also supervise lesser angels – they give orders to angels without charges and assign charges to new guardians. However, the Principalities are under the authority of angels from the first two spheres; they receive orders from above and execute them or transmit them to lower angels. In short, they're the messengers of the hierarchy, acting as intermediaries between different spheres. The Principalities are depicted as humans with a scepter in their hands and a crown on their heads.

The next order belongs to the Archangels, the angelic chieftains who look over a group of angels. They're widely known as they can appear to everyone and assist with different tasks, depending on what's needed in any given situation. They can travel between realms, often being present in several worlds simultaneously. Each Archangel has certain specialties. However, they are also divine messengers. The number of recognized Archangels varies from four to nine or more, depending on which belief system you're consulting. Metatron is an Archangel only recognized by some religions.

All the rest of the angels fill the lowest order. These are beings present in people's lives in one form or another. Some angels have guardian roles – they have a human charge assigned to them, and they guide this person from birth to death. The order of Angels is further broken down into smaller categories based on the roles of the angels. For instance, some angels are in charge of nature, while others are tied to emotions. Everything and everyone ever created has an angel. The wisdom of angels in this order is limited to their functions. Even guardians that guide and protect their charges have limited powers. However, your guardian is the closest to you and is more likely to receive your call if you need angelic guidance.

The Role of Metatron in the Angelic Spheres

Now that you've familiarized yourself with the angelic hierarchy system, you can explore Metatron and his celestial role and place in the spheres. Metatron is one of the most powerful beings in the angelic kingdom, so it's no surprise that he has several roles across the spheres. Often called the "Divine Chancellor" or the "Divine Scribe," Metatron is in charge of recording everything happening on Earth. This function ties him to the concept called the "Book of Life," a record listing the names of people worthy of salvation.

Besides recording people's actions (and their consequences), Metatron also carries divine messages to people. He also distributes divine will to angelic beings. Moreover, he establishes communication between the angelic and earthly realms by creating a bridge through divine messages.

Last but not least, Metatron is responsible for aiding the souls of the deceased on their journey toward their final destination. Known as the "Archangel of Death," Metatron ensures that souls find peace in the afterlife. This is what Metatron is most revered for in many traditions and belief systems.

Metatron's Origins

There are references to the origins of Metatron in many mystical texts, including The Zohar, Talmud, and Book of Enoch, to name a few. While the origins of Metatron can only be established based on mystical texts, Hebrew mythology provides a relatively rich source to explain and understand where Archangel Metatron comes from. The Jewish Tanakh describes Metatron as an enigmatic character with the role of a divine messenger. According to this source, Metatron is responsible for transmitting heavenly edicts to both people and angels. He even passes heavenly orders on to other Archangels like Raphael and Gabriel, with whom he communicates daily.

Other sources trace the origins of Metatron back to the day when the Jewish people were led from Egypt to Israel, claiming that it was Metatron who provided the guidance they needed to reach their destination. Interestingly enough, while Metatron isn't mentioned in the New Testament or the Tanakh, Metatron is recognized by some branches of Christianity and Judaism. These belief systems list him under the names of Metator, Metraton, and Mattatron.

The name of Archangel Metatron has unclear roots as well. Different religions assign different etymologies to his name. For example, some assert that Metatron's name is derived from the Greek phrase that translates as "the one behind the throne." While this seems to be a popular definition, it's also the least probable. A far more accepted translation for Metatron's name comes from the Hebrew term that translates as "the guardian of entryways." This is probably because Metatron is mostly known from Hebrew myths, making it more believable that his name also has Hebrew origins. There is also a third possible etymology of Metatron's name. This one comes from the Latin words "*mitator*," which means "explorer of legions," and "*metator*," which is defined as a messenger.

It's also interesting to note that Metatron is one of the two Archangels whose name ends with an "-on," which means "great." The only other Archangel whose name ends with an "-on" is Metatron's brother, Sandalfon. The meaning of the "on" ending is first referenced in the Book of Enoch, a tome later edited in the 1st century B.C. Two centuries later, the Book of Enoch was edited again, which led to different versions of the concepts and participants it describes, including the Archangel Metatron.

In the initial version, Metraton was referred to as one of the most influential beings in the celestial realm – evidenced by the fact he was usually portrayed sitting on the Creator's left. However, later versions claimed that because he sat on the left and the Creator's Son on the right, Metatron represented an opposing force to the Son – equating him with Lucifer, the adversary of the divine. This is also tied to the version that myths claim that Metatron was the oldest of the Archangels; in the third version of the Book of Enoch, Metatron's origins as a human was born. According to this version, the Archangel was a wealthy prophet named Enoch. Precisely because of how many versions of Metatron are in Hebrew mythology and other belief systems, certain branches of Christianity refuse to recognize him as an Archangel. There were just too many different narratives about Metatron, making it challenging to find a cohesive one that fit certain Christian beliefs.

Despite this, he is referenced in many other religions and traditions. The earliest tangible reference comes from the Talmud, a fundamental source of teachings of Rabbinic Judaism. Here, Metatron is portrayed as the most prominent figure in the history of the religion. The Talmud's reference to the angel's role in leading the Israelites from Egypt also allowed Metatron to become a widely known character in Jewish mysticism. Metatron's essence began infiltrating this belief system around the end of the 12th and the beginning of the 13th centuries, when many Kabbalistic theories were born. While these are different from traditional Jewish beliefs, followers still found Metatron to be necessary as they transitioned to the Kabbalistic beliefs. According to these, Metatron (originally referred to as Enoch) is viewed as someone Jews could rely on when they rejected Christ. They turned to Enoch in defiance as he was a human, but they later "converted" him into a higher being. This explains why Kabbalistic beliefs view Metatron as the second most powerful being (after the Creator).

The belief that Metatron was a scribe angel asserts that this angel possesses divine wisdom. Through this wisdom, he can open the doors to cosmic secrets and empower one's spirituality through daily practices. This is illustrated by the image portraying him with eyes all over his being. It's said that he has 365,000 eyes – the number of days in the year multiplied by the totality of his meanings. Some claim that this number also indicates the totality of time. Whereas others believe the numerous eyes symbolize his elevated consciousness. After all, he is known to be clairvoyant and can always predict what is to come.

The Epithets and Attributes of Metatron

The Kabbalah, a form of Jewish mysticism, plays a crucial role in understanding some key attributes of Metatron. Revolving around the Tree of Life concept, this belief system directly ties Metatron to the symbolic representation of the universe's divine structure. The Tree of Life incorporates ten spheres (known as sefirot, or sefirah in singular), all interconnected. The spheres depict different facets of the divine. The highest sefirah, Keter, embodies divine will. It represents the source of all creation and is linked to Metatron. This makes this angel the highest-ranking being in the Kabbalistic belief system. Due to his connection to the divine will, Metatron is also known as "the lesser YHVH." In the Kabbalah, Metatron transmits divine energy through the Tree of Life, allowing it to trickle down to people. While this role seems to lessen Metatron's role in Kabbalistic practices, his influence over the entire celestial hierarchy is undeniable. After all, he is the only angel who can channel divine energy.

One of Metatron's most well-known symbols, the Metatron's Cube, is believed to be modeled after the Tree of Life. However, other Kabbalistic sources claim that Metatron molded this symbol from his own soul, so it is often portrayed as an entity closely connected to the angel floating near him.

Metatron's connection to the divine is also evident in his role as the celestial messenger. He can communicate divine edicts to people and angels because he has access to them. He can also record them and all the information needed to maintain cosmic balance. Metatron is said to record all this information in the "Book of Life," the ultimate source of divine knowledge. Not only is he in close quarters with the divine, but he is also endowed with transformative and healing powers. An example of his powers is seen in his role as the "Highest Angel of Death," which entails guiding souls through the afterlife and ensuring they reach their destination.

Another interesting epithet of Metatron is his role in guarding children – a belief that originates from Metatron's portrayal in Zohar. Here, Metatron is also praised for his role in safely guiding the children of Israel to the Promised Land and across the treacherous desert. Because of this feat, a myth of Metatron guides children in all realms to overcome obstacles they face in life as they transition through the different stages. It is said that parents can call on Metatron to ensure their children's spiritual and academic development and also to help them hone their intuitive abilities. Metatron will hear the parent's inquiries and guide the children toward the right path. Some say that Metatron will also continue to lead children in the heavenly realm should they pass on. Other sources claim that Metatron helps children develop their communication skills and can be particularly helpful for troubled youth struggling with neurodevelopmental disorders. Besides helping children resolve their health and social issues, Metatron can empower parents and those around them, guiding them on the best path to overcome obstacles. Health professionals and scientists working with children also consider Metatron as their patron. Whether he does it on the earth or in the heavenly realm, it's clear that Metatron aims to help children adapt to their environment. He is believed to be a great source of self-esteem, focus, and spiritual awareness for children and adults concerned with children's fates alike.

Metatron's Connection with Enoch

There are many theories about the different aspects of Metatron, including the one that connects him with Enoch – the human incarnation of Metatron. In the Third Book of Enoch, Metatron is clearly identified as Enoch in several parts. For example, Enoch (an ancient patriarch and son of Jared) is given the title "The lesser YHVH" when he describes "the Holy One," referencing him by this name.

Being a righteous man all his life, Enoch was taken to the heavenly realm to appear before the Creator before his death. He walked and talked with the Creator, journeying through the heavenly realms, and eventually transformed into an Archangel. Enoch's transformation from a biblical figure to a celestial being known as Metatron is certainly one of the most intriguing stories surrounding this angel. However, Enoch had to undergo several trials before becoming an angel.

A paragraph illustrates how flames suddenly engulfed Enoch; his veins turned into fire, and his eyes lit up with flashes of lightning as he was elevated by the divine next to his throne of glory. This clearly references Enoch's transformation into Metatron and ascension into the angelic realm. The First Book of Enoch also references Metatron's connection. For instance, it describes the Lord giving an edict to Enoch (addressing him as "The Scribe of Righteousness"). This edict declares to "the Watchers of heaven," who abandoned their duties, gave in to the earthly temptations, and brought great destruction to themselves and those around them on the earth.

Enoch's transformation into Metatron is pivotal in Jewish traditions. It points out that Metatron was once an ordinary human living a mundane life. While this sets him apart from the other Archangels, it's also a testimony to his worthiness to stand close to the divine. He was chosen to stand by the Creator while he was still a human and was allowed to gain a prominent position in the heavenly kingdom after his transformation. Last but not least, Enoch's transformation into an Archangel indicates that people have tremendous potential for spiritual growth. Through spiritual development, everyone can ascend to a higher spiritual plane. Human experiences are necessary for ascension as they teach people many crucial lessons.

Archangel Metatron or Archangel Michael?

While many belief systems clearly distinguish between Archangel Metatron and Archangel Michael, some argue that the two embody the same angelic energy, appearing in different forms. However, historical evidence and mystical texts with several references to the distinct roles of both Archangel Metatron and Archangel Michael indicate that they are not the same figure. For example, in Zohar, in religious traditions and customs, Archangel Metatron is represented by the "Tent of the Congregation," empowering its structure. On the other hand, Michael is embodied by the High Priest, who communicates divine messages to the congregation. For Hebrews, Metatron is a multifaceted being, but he has a distinct role in bringing souls to the presence of the divine, while Archangel Michael has a role in the protection of the soul. He is also more active in combating negativity, while Metatron is known for his peaceful energy. Although there are many similarities between them, they also have different statuses. Archangel Michael is the defender, the "heavenly Prince," as opposed to the "God's scribe," as Archangel Metatron is widely known. Some also claim that because Michael is named in the Bible and Metatron isn't, this also proves that they aren't the same being.

Different roles notwithstanding, Metatron has a unique relationship with Archangel Michael. As another prominent figure in the angelic hierarchy, Archangel Michael serves a role in a divine plan intended for Metatron. Some claim that the transformative powers of Metatron wouldn't be accessible to anyone without the protective guardianship of a warrior Archangel like Michael. Whether this is true or not, several religious and mystical traditions testify to the significant relationship between Archangel Michael and Metatron. One of the parallels between the myths surrounding these two high-ranking celestial beings comes from the stories describing their connection to Enoch. As described in the "Book of Enoch," Enoch was a biblical figure who recorded roles in the angelic hierarchy after visiting the heavenly realm – including the roles he shared and fulfilled in tandem with Archangel Michael.

Moreover, the connection between these two angels is required to maintain the heavenly order. They have ties to the divine essence and do their best to fulfill their roles as intermediaries between the angelic and earth realms and their inhabitants.

Chapter 2: Ascension with Metatron

Given Metatron's connection to Enoch, it's safe to say this celestial being has been through an incredible spiritual transformation when ascending to the heavenly realm. And because of his ascension, Metatron can be a powerful ally for those seeking their spiritual transformation. This chapter will introduce you to the concept of ascension. It analyzes personal ascension, including its steps (abusive past release, raising energy levels and awareness, and others), and how you can achieve them through the connection with Metatron. You'll learn how much time is needed for this procedure and the benefits of completing it. You'll also be given a practical guide (with easy-to-do steps) to achieve personal ascension, along with tips on recognizing whether the process has taken place on physical or spiritual levels.

Personal Ascension

Personal ascension is defined as becoming a newer, better version of oneself. It's a gradual process that starts with slowly increasing self-awareness until you become fully awakened. It's unique (and personal) – a journey you must take by yourself, although you can call on some reinforcements along the way. Because ascension is also confusing and sometimes even painful at first, you need guidance to recognize whether you're on the right path and shift your consciousness toward a better understanding of why and how you need to ascend.

People change all the time. Ascension just makes sure it's for the better. It makes a shift within you, enabling you to manifest positive changes outside as well. It allows you to grow spiritually and personally, discard unwanted ties and release unhealthy thoughts and relationships. It helps you gain insight and self-realization. Sometimes, you get drawn to new ideas and start making new choices that benefit your spiritual journey. You gain a new perspective of the world as a whole and a deeper understanding of how to make it a better place for yourself and those around you.

Here are the basic steps of spiritual awakening and ascension:
1. Encountering darkness after realizing that what you know about your life isn't true.
2. Finding hope when you break through spiritual bonds as you let go of past hurts.
3. Building inquisitiveness – reaching into your intuition for spiritual answers.
4. Facing inner conflict when your spiritual self-confronts your ego self.
5. Experiencing spiritual transformation through higher awareness and raising your vibrations.
6. Spiritual bypassing – unwillingness to delve into and ignore the deeper hurts.
7. Grounding, further raising your energies, and realizing that the only way to move on is to heal from everything – including hurts you haven't explored yet.
8. Opening up to your past and present experiences, bringing awareness to your spiritual needs and desires.
9. Finding and embracing your soul's purpose.
10. Mastering spiritual lessons about enlightenment and becoming the best version of your spiritual self.

Metatron is the Archangel of transformation. If you need help with spiritual development, he is the best guide to call upon. He can teach you how to gain confidence, start your journey of awakening, and recognize the signs that your ascension is upon you. He can accompany you on your journey to discover your own personal and spiritual power. He can help you uncover your power and serve you and this universe's greater good.

You might be wondering why Metatron is your best ally in personal ascension. This Archangel is closely linked to the energy of the solar plexus chakra, your energetic center responsible for strengthening your sense of self. This chakra can be a great source of personal power and self-mastery. Its energy is also linked to co-creative pursuits. Tapping into it will help you build healthy relationships with people around you and connect to higher beings. It allows you to establish boundaries and challenge the divine energy the angels gift you.

Metatron is the source of wisdom that will help you discover and realize your soul's purpose in this life – through spiritual awakening and ascension. All Archangels have specialties – Metatron's is ascension through spiritual empowerment. He can help you empower yourself by bringing forth information you've kept in the depths of your soul. Some of this information might be painful to re-discover, but it's part of a healing process. And when you heal from past traumas, you start living a more fulfilled life. This, in turn, enables you to find your purpose. Regardless of how deep or old your spiritual wounds are, they can affect your spiritual health in the present and future. Some believe that Archangel Metatron can help heal traumas from past lives – traumas so hurtful that they bleed through one's current life.

Whether your practice or beliefs include reaching into past lives or not, when you need to heal distant traumas, if you call on him, Archangel Metatron will help you. He can help you make the connection between past events and current complications in your life. Besides guiding you, Metatron also points you in the direction of personal spirit guides who will work closely with you, empowering your life and spirit and facilitating its ascension to its highest purpose.

Metatron has one of the highest vibrational energies in the universe. If you want to release or remove energetic blocks and heal your energies, the best way to start is to raise your vibrations. And who better to help you boost your vibes than someone who has experienced his own elevation and knows all the benefits of aligning one's vibrations with the highest power?

Metatron is a master channeler of energies. He can help direct your energies toward the right path and harness the power of whoever you find empowerment in. Whether you want to channel the energy of your spirit guides, guardian angels, or your higher self, Archangel Metatron can show you the way.

Metatron is just interested in discovering your soul's hidden desires as you are. Once you establish a connection with him, Metatron will encourage you to get to know your soul. It will also help him learn more about you to provide better guidance in researching your soul and uncovering everything you need to know about it, good or bad. Whatever you find, Metatron will point out that only your overall spiritual personality counts. If you start working on both sides of your soul, the good soon shines through the bad, and you'll have clarity on who your spiritual self is and what you can do for it. Metatron loves to assist in this process because he knows it helps you uncover your soul's characteristics, which is the most critical step in spiritual awakening. The experiences you choose to have and why you chose them from this point on will build a foundation for a self-fulfillment journey that leads to personal ascension.

Archangel Metatron is linked to the higher states of consciousness. By teaching you how to achieve these states one by one, he facilitates spiritual growth and awakening and helps your soul ascend. He can send you the signs you need to unlock your soul for growth and elevate it to higher levels. He will push you forward to become a fully expanded and enlightened conscious version of your spiritual self. Metatron will activate energies that raise your vibration to their fullest power and boost psychic and intuitive development. You will become far more receptive to spiritual messages when you improve your connection with your intuition. Deciphering spiritual messages and aligning your life with their advice is one of the best ways to propel spiritual growth. Besides your solar plexus chakra, Metatron is also associated with your crown chakra. This energetic center oversees and fills all your other chakras with higher energies. As you embrace your intuitive powers, you're opening your crown chakra, allowing Metatron to empower your spiritual being with his energy.

Signs That Your Ascension Is Taking Place

Feeling content for no reason can be a sign of personal ascension.
https://www.pexels.com/photo/woman-wearing-white-sleeveless-lace-shirt-935985/

There are many different indicators of personal ascension. Here are some of the signs that you are arriving at your true nature and have begun your journey toward ascension to the divine:

- You feel your heart opening to others, to all of nature, to yourself; forgiveness and understanding come with ease for yourself and for others
- Raised consciousness and alignment with your conscious self
- A feeling of oneness with the universe and nature
- Developing psychic powers, like telepathy with those around you
- You feel the need to be of service—not in what you do but to do something for others in general
- You feel the freedom that comes with following your path and inner guidance, and you are not constricted by the rules of society
- Trust in the divine – and that everything will work out just fine.
- Seeing beauty in everything and everyone allows your focus on it everything and anything to expand

- Feeling joy and happiness for no apparent reason
- Feeling your authentic self and knowing your soul is the greatest gift you ever received
- Awareness of light – seeing it in nature, other people's souls, etc.
- Feeling lighter – The more you release the old energies that wear you out, the lighter you start to feel
- Awareness of love and other people's soul.
- Ability to let go of judgment and separate your true consciousness from mundane thoughts
- Being able to unconditionally love, accept and forgive yourself and those who hurt you in the past
- Feelings of divine grace – almost as if it would carry you in a state of weightlessness, embracing you with unconditional love and being able to go with the flow
- Gaining the ability to be present – here – now and openly channel peace and awareness in your mind and spirit
- Seeing how your past dissolves behind you, and you cease worrying about your future. You are letting it all go and focusing on being present.
- Taking care of yourself: physically, emotionally, mentally, and spiritually. Loving and honoring yourself
- Recognizing the multidimensionality of your consciousness

Establishing the First Contact

Delving into the practical side of ascension with Metatron, your first step is establishing contact with this Archangel. Here is a simple invocation to make the first call to him:

> *"Metatron, I ask you to join me now,*
> *And request and trust your guidance for my spiritual journey.*
> *I ask you to infuse your wisdom and energy into my being,*
> *So I can ascend and reach my soul's highest potential,*
> *And my journey of expansion and learning will be fruitful.*
> *I ask you to help me to tap into my higher self,*
> *So I can receive the guidance I need to ascend my spirit.*
> *Please join me now and raise my energy with your powers."*

Metatron Mantras

Mantras are a combination of words infused with your energy. Your words can have immense power and help manifest your intentions to ascend your soul. Using mantras can also be a great way to invite Archangel Metatron to join you on your ascension journey.

Here are a few mantras you can repeat while calling on Metatron:

I am guided by the magnificent Archangel Metatron today.
I know Metatron is helping me to ascend my spirit.
I am surrounded by the loving energy of Archangel Metatron.
Archangel Metatron is opening my intuition.
I am one with Metatron and the divine energy.
The angelic light of Archangel Metatron courses through me.
I am connected to Metatron's light and angelic essence.
My trusty guide, Archangel Metatron, is ascending my spirit.

Metatron Meditation

Meditation can help you establish a connection with Metatron.
Photo by Marcus Aurelius: https://www.pexels.com/photo/woman-practicing-yoga-6787217/

The following Metatron meditation will help you establish a deeper connection with this archangel. It will also be a great practice in grounding and working on your intuition.

Instructions:
1. Find a comfortable position at a place where you won't be disturbed. Close your eyes and focus on your breath.
2. Deepen your breathing by gently expanding your abdomen with each inhalation. As you feel your stomach expanding, do your best to release your thoughts.
3. When your mind is freed of your thoughts, take a deep breath - inhale until your abdomen can't expand anymore.
4. You will feel pressure on your solar plexus chakra - this is the force of your inner power, don't fight it. Take a moment to embrace this and release your breath.
5. Next, feel as if your power begins to rise. Connect to that essence by first focusing on the sensations in your head. This will bring your attention to your crown and third eye chakras.
6. Imagine a purple light coming from your third eye chakra, traveling upwards to your crown chakra, and swirling up to the sky. Feel parts of yourself traveling up with this light higher and higher until you reach the highest plane, the source of universal wisdom.
7. Feel your connection to the universal wisdom and the vastness of the universe. Now imagine a bright star appearing in front of you. As it approaches you, it reaches out to you with a beam of bright energy.
8. As you think about where this energy comes from, you suddenly see Archangel Metatron. Feel free to greet him with the following words:

    "Metatron, the brightest of the Archangels.
    I am honored to meet you.
    Please introduce me to your loving guidance.
    My mind is open to receiving your infinite wisdom.
    And I am forever grateful for your multidimensional energy.
    I ask you to show me the depth of my power

> *Shine your light on my soul so my purpose becomes clear now.*
>
> *Thank you, Archangel Metatron."*

9. If you have a personal message to send to Archangel Metatron, deliver it now.
10. Imagine Metatron offering you his hand and inviting you to join him under his brightly lit aura. Take a few moments to enjoy the archangel's support.
11. When you're ready, gently open your eyes and let your thought slowly fill your mind again.

Releasing Past with Archangel Metatron

The following deep meditation will clear and align your energy by releasing past energetic influences. It will also bring you closer to Archangel Metatron and his incredibly powerful energy, allowing you to tap into his wisdom. This will help you transform aspects of your life. Practicing this exercise teaches you to cultivate your inner self and share Metatron's unconditional love and angelic energy with those around you. It's an excellent method to deeply purge and release old, unhealthy ties, situations, or relationships from your life.

Instructions:

1. Find a comfortable place to sit, close your eyes, and take a few deep breaths.
2. Imagine a beam of sparkling white light emerging from the earth underneath your feet. See it traveling upwards into your feet, legs, stomach, and back and reaching your arms and, ultimately, your head.
3. Feel how this light fills you with energy and call on Archangel Metatron by chanting his name three times and asking him to join you now. Make this request from your heart. Repeat it if necessary.
4. Take a few deep breaths and imagine how the energy coursing through you becomes even stronger. Imagine expanding it, sending it out as far as it can go – through the universe.
5. Notice how you feel at one with the space you've sent the energy. Feel joined with Metatron's energy. His aura feels like a warm, comfortable blanket.

6. Metatron's energy feels light because he only seeks your highest good. Trust his power, let go and allow your body to absorb his energy.
7. Allow Metatron to explore your energy field to find any troubles or energetic blocks. You can also confide in him about any issues you had with any aspect of your life (if you have conscious knowledge of them).
8. Now imagine Metatron's sparkling bright light reaching all the areas of your life (good or bad) and expanding them, enlightening them with transformative light.
9. Feel your entire body expanding with Metatron's sparkling life, reaching out to your environment. Imagine the energy reaching out to the loved ones you want to protect and empower.
10. Next, channel your attention to your energy. Let the previous image go. Once again, see the universal energy travel up toward your feet and reach every part of your body. You might feel it more intensely now because Metatron is guiding you.
11. As you feel energy reaching different areas of your body, focus on the sensation you feel in each of them. Pay attention to any negative feelings because these can be sources of bad energy.
12. Let the energy swirl around you to ensure it catches all the negativity and unwanted energies in your entire system. As it does, you'll feel lighter, safer, more loved, and happier.
13. When the energy reaches your head, feel how it eliminates any emotional and spiritual debris that doesn't belong there. You have energy with incredibly high vibrations coursing through you now. Allow it to purge all stale and old energy from your life.
14. Imagine a beam of sparkling light reaching into your heart chakra, clearing out past traumas, and releasing everything that hurt your heart and soul.
15. When you can feel only gratitude for all the blessings you've received and none of the resentment that comes with past hurt, you're now free of everything that no longer serves you.
16. Take a deep breath, allow your renewed energy to expand toward the universe, and ask Metatron to continue working with you to reach your highest potential.

17. Thank Metatron for his assistance, and when you are ready, imagine bringing your energy back to you. See it form a bubble of light around you, containing protective energy around you.
18. When you're ready, you can return to your thoughts.

Raising Vibrations

When you work with Archangel Metatron, you're reciting a large dose of high-frequency vibrational ascension. Below, you'll find a quick but powerful exercise to connect you to the energy of Archangel Metatron and clear your energy.

Instructions:

1. After assuming a comfortable position, close your eyes and focus on your breath.
2. As you relax, imagine roots coming out from your feet. They're then developed by a bright light that travels up to your core.
3. The light fills you with energy you can extend – because it *vibrates at a higher frequency.*
4. As you expand the energy, take a couple of deep breaths and ask Archangel Metatron to join you. Allow him to tap into your energetic field and work with you on upgrading it.
5. Feel how he elevates your vibrations and cuts all unwanted ties from your life.
6. You're now filled with even more light and energy that vibrates so highly you never thought it possible. Yet you feel safe because you know that having this energy in you is beneficial for you.
7. Take a few deep breaths and allow Metatron's light to fill your mind, body, and soul. Feel how your energies are bringing you closer to Metatron's. This is a sign that your vibrations are being raised.
8. Imagine the Archangel Metatron creating a protective shield around you, containing your energy and vibrations at a higher level.
9. Slowly let the image go and let your thoughts return to you.

Chapter 3: Recognizing Metatron's Presence

Metatron is watching over you. When you seek his guidance and reach out to him, he will answer your call. For some people, this can happen right away, while for others, it can take some time. However, you have to believe that he will eventually respond. Angels don't usually send direct messages and can't appear to you in their true form because they vibrate at different frequencies. Therefore, they will announce their presence through specific symbols. If you aren't familiar with these signs, you will not notice when an angel is present and miss the messages they are trying to communicate to you.

In this chapter, you will discover the different signs and symbols associated with Metatron so you can recognize the angel's presence.

Colors

Metatron has a colorful aura, and he is associated with white, dark green, pink, blue, and red. Each of these colors has a meaning behind it. Once you learn them, you can decipher the angel's message to you.

White

The color white indicates that tough times are passing.
https://www.pexels.com/photo/texture-wall-white-colors-1843717/

The color white indicates that you are going through a tough time, but things are about to improve. You may be facing problems in your personal life, like a bad breakup or family issues. Metatron can send you this color as a message of hope to tell you to be patient because good things are coming.

Green

The color green represents healing or truth.
https://unsplash.com/photos/eB1ziPSixlQ?utm_source=unsplash&utm_medium=referral&utm_content=creditShareLink

The color green has multiple meanings; it represents healing, honesty, or truth. If Metatron sends you a green color or green flashes of light, it can be a sign that you are about to heal from your pain. It can also signify that the truth you seek is about to be revealed.

Pink

Seeing a pink light might indicate that you've been neglecting yourself.
https://unsplash.com/photos/z4n8CGRuzOA?utm_source=unsplash&utm_medium=referral&utm_content=creditShareLink

Seeing a pink color or light indicates you should restore balance in your life and relationships. It can also be a reminder that you have been neglecting yourself. Real empowerment comes from self-love, so you should make yourself a priority. Metatron is telling you to take care of your well-being and the people in your life. Nourishing your relationships can contribute to your personal growth, but you cannot love and support others until you learn to value yourself.

Blue

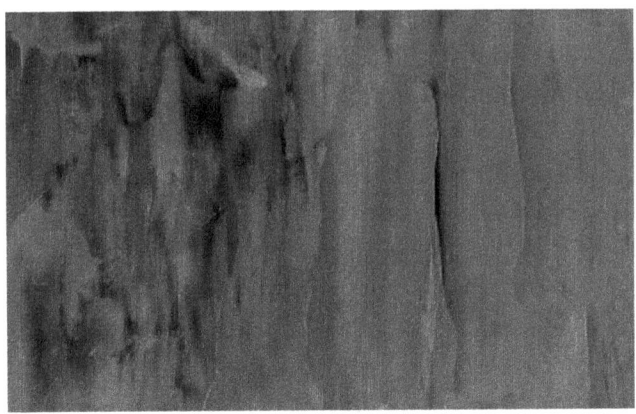

Blue indicates that you have potential.
https://unsplash.com/photos/dVRD8E3XUGs?utm_source=unsplash&utm_medium=referral&utm_content=creditShareLink

Blue is associated with motivation and encouragement. When you receive this message, it means you have potential and can achieve your goals, so start working on them right away. It is a sign that you should start believing in your abilities and have the power and courage to show your true self to the world. The angel is trying to tell you not to be afraid to open yourself up because this is the only way you will receive what the universe is ready to give you.

Red

Seeing red can indicate that you're facing stress.
https://unsplash.com/photos/Ar6eXpQaCwk?utm_source=unsplash&utm_medium=referral&utm_content=creditShareLink

Metatron will send red flashes or colors your way when you face conflict, stress, or anxiety in your daily life. The purpose of this message is to urge you to calm the noise in your head. It is time to make peace with those who hurt you and forget your painful past. You should let go of your guilt and forgive yourself for all your mistakes.

The main purpose of Metatron's signs is to get your attention. He wants to tell you that he is present and has a message for you so his symbols will be loud and clear. You will keep seeing the same color everywhere you go until you notice it and look for its meaning.

For instance, you can keep seeing blue cars every day on your way to work. When you arrive at the office, you see your boss or any of your co-workers wearing a blue suit, and when you get home in the evening, you find your partner bringing you a blue sweater as a gift or your children or pets playing with blue toys. Simply put, the color will take over your life. All these events aren't coincidences; you are receiving a message from your angel.

Dreams

Metatron can come to you in a dream to warn you against an impending danger or let you know he is right here with you. He can appear to you as a white light or in any different form. However, you will be able to recognize him because you are already connected.

Courage

Everyone experiences fear; it is one of the most common emotions in the world. However, this feeling can bring negative thoughts and energies that stop you from reaching your potential and achieving your goals. Metatron will replace your fears with courage and confidence when he is present. You will start believing in your talents, abilities, and skills and seeing yourself differently.

Remember that Metatron's presence is empowering. He will give you the courage to face the unknown when he is near you, and your limitations will no longer control you.

Geometric Patterns

Seeing geometric patterns is a sign of Metatron's presence.
https://unsplash.com/photos/OxHPDs4WV8Y?utm_source=unsplash&utm_medium=referral&utm_content=creditShareLink

Suppose you keep seeing squares, triangles, circles, 3D objects, or any other shape in random places. In that case, these are all signs of Metatron's presence.

Intuition

Once you reach out to Metatron, look for his messages immediately. Believe that he will eventually respond and start searching for opportunities and meanings in every random event and person you meet. Since angels can't directly communicate with you, they will send you people or specific situations to convey their message.

For instance, you have a job interview tomorrow at a reputable company and are very excited about it. Out of nowhere, your cousin, whom you haven't spoken to in months, calls you. While you are catching up, she tells you about her last job and how her boss ruined her life. She tells you that working in this place is her biggest regret, but she is grateful to get out and put this horrible experience behind her. When you ask her about the company's name, you discover that this is the same place you are having your interview tomorrow.

You are grateful for your cousin's phone call and decide that you will not go to the interview. You probably think that this is a coincidence. However, this is the work of Metatron. He sent your cousin to warn you against going to this interview.

Metatron will reach out to you in different ways, so listen to your intuition and focus on your impulses. You can have the urge to do something or a gut feeling to steer clear of a situation. Your angel is showing you the right path and nudging you toward your destiny. He will put people in your way to inspire you to reach your goals or warn you against things that aren't right for you.

Make Peace with Your Past

Since Metatron has access to the Akashic Records, which contain your memories and past mistakes, he can influence you to deal with your past issues and traumas so you can make peace with them. He will bring all the emotions you are afraid of to the surface so you can face them and deal with them.

These records will be discussed in detail in the coming chapters.

Paintings

In paintings, Metatron is often depicted as a guardian standing next to the tree of life, keeping it safe. He usually wears a pink, green, or blue robe and has golden wings. Randomly seeing this image in paintings or pictures is a sign of his presence.

Processing Emotions

If you have been processing your emotions differently lately, this indicates that Metatron is close to you. In the long run, his presence will inspire you to reach your higher self and learn how to express your emotions properly. This change in your personality will not happen immediately; it will take time, but eventually, you will experience real transformation. Metatron is by your side, pushing you to become the best version of yourself.

Number Eleven

You have probably been told to make a wish at 11:11, as this is a special time. 11:11 indicates that a gateway is open, giving you access to the spiritual world.

The number eleven is associated with Metatron. If you constantly see it in this specific form, 11:11, the angel is present and providing guidance. It can also be a message of validation.

Eleven is also a sign that something amazing is about to happen in your life. You can see it on buses, tickets, your cell phone, or digital clocks. The number also indicates that you are experiencing a spiritual awakening. If you are struggling with a decision, this sign encourages you to take a leap of faith.

Although 11:11 is usually open to many interpretations because each person relates it to something different depending on their own experiences, it is always associated with Metatron and the spiritual world.

When you see this number, pay attention to your life and goals and assess what needs to be done or changed to achieve them. Metatron is by your side, guiding you every step of the way.

It can also be a reassuring sign to remind you that you aren't alone and that Metatron will always be here for you. If you have asked him about ascension, he can send you this number to give you the answers you seek.

Numbers are usually the most common symbols angels use to communicate with human beings.

Scents

When Metatron is near, you will experience strong and unusual scents of spices and herbs, like peppercorns, chilies, or sweet floral smells. You wake up every day smelling an unusual fragrance. It is in your car, on your way to work at your office, and everywhere you go. The scent is taking over your life.

Sounds

Auditory signs are often the easiest to recognize. You may miss colors or scents, but it is impossible not to notice a loud noise. When Metatron is near, you can hear a high-pitched buzzing sound in your left ear. In some cases, you can also hear him speak in a low and soft voice.

Tingling in the Chakras

When Metatron wants to announce his presence or communicate with you, he will activate your seventh chakra (crown chakra), located on top of your head. It is associated with divine communication and spiritual elevation. You will experience higher awareness and spiritual energy revealing the answers you have sought about yourself or the universe.

Thoughts Shifting

Since Metatron is meant to empower you, he can influence you to change your thought pattern. Say you have been having negative thoughts lately, but suddenly, you have the urge to replace them with positive and happy ones. This means the angel is with you and working on eliminating the negativity from your life.

Metatron is the keeper of the universe's records; this gives him insight into the human mind. He knows how people's negative thoughts can impact their lives. He is curious about how they think, and he has seen that positive individuals lead happy and healthy lives while negative ones are miserable and constantly struggle to make healthy and good decisions.

When Metatron is present, he will inspire you to focus on your thoughts and to choose positivity over negativity. He wants to remind you that you are in control of your mind, not the other way around. You have the power to alter your pattern of thoughts so you can think positively and change your life.

Metatron's presence will elevate your consciousness and fill your mind with creative ideas. Your thoughts will inspire and motivate you to make better choices and live your best life. This is a clear sign that Metatron is by your side, guiding you and inspiring you to think positively.

White Light

Metatron can send you flashes of white light to let you know he is here. You will easily notice this sign since the light will be strong and almost blinding. Metatron's vibrational frequency is higher than any other angle, so his fiery presence is always noticeable. He can also manifest in any colors associated with him, like blue, green, and pink.

Personal Experience

Many people have encountered Metatron at one time or another during their lives. The last part of the chapter will narrate the personal experience of a young girl who communicated with the angel.

Elizabeth was connected with Metatron and knew he was her guide. She constantly saw many signs from him; he appeared in her dreams, and she was always drawn to him. One night, Elizabeth was meditating and saw herself standing in front of a cathedral door in heaven. She knew Metatron was on the other side and was nervous. The angel waited for her to enter; he didn't want to rush her. She opened the door, walked in, and sat beside him. Elizabeth didn't say a word because she was overwhelmed by the experience. However, Metatron welcomed her and expressed his joy that she had found him. He explained to her that her negative thoughts weren't her fault and they shouldn't define her. She was strong and had power over her darkness, and he asked her to forgive herself.

Elizabeth hugged Metatron, and she could feel his unconditional love for her. However, she was overwhelmed by her emotions and broke down in tears. The angel comforted her and told her he wasn't going anywhere.

She asked him to show her who she was in a past life, and he complied. In the vision, Metatron was standing behind her. He told her he was always with her in every life she experienced. Metatron explained that he would have her back and constantly watch over her forever. He then took her to an oak tree, and they sat in silence.

In her experience, Metatron didn't have a face. He was a tall light with long hair and wearing a purple robe.

In life, there are no coincidences. If you encounter strange events, don't brush them off because there is always a meaning behind them. Metatron can manifest himself to you in different ways. However, you will never recognize his messages if you don't pay attention.

Understand the meaning behind everything you experience. Suppose you keep smelling a strange scent, seeing the number eleven everywhere you go, or seeing geometric patterns. In that case, this can indicate that Metatron is near you.

You are the only person who can decipher Metatron's signs when he reaches out to you. Although his symbols can have general meanings, the hidden message behind them is personal. For instance, if you feel alone and Metatron sends you the number eleven, he lets you know he is with you. For someone else, the number can provide guidance.

You and your angel share a special bond, so even if the messages can seem strange or unclear to someone else, you will know what they mean.

When you call out for Metatron, keep all your senses open and prepare yourself for all the messages you are about to receive. Metatron can be by your side right now, and you don't even know it, *so stay focused.*

Chapter 4: Metatron's Cube

In many religions and spiritual belief systems, God is credited with having created the entire universe with a unique geometric plan. This is why most people consider geometrical shapes to be sacred and symbolic of some underlying divine message and is how the concept of sacred geometry came into being. If you think about it, the principles of geometry govern the very essence of this universe. The patterns, proportions, frequencies, ratios, and geometric shapes underlie any organic life forms, objects, and phenomena in the universe. Many people revere sacred geometry symbols for this exact reason and try to use them to understand and interpret the divine truths behind all existence. One of these revered shapes is Metatron's cube.

If you're interested in the healing and empowering strength of the Archangel Metatron, you've probably heard of Metatron's cube and how it plays into spiritually connecting with the Archangel. This divine and complex structure is considered one of the most sacred geometric patterns in existence in history. The Archangel Metatron oversees the energy flow in this sacred cube, which encompasses every geometric shape and structure in this universe. Metatron's cube is said to be derived from the ancient structure of the flower of life. It is the perfect blueprint of cosmic creation, an architecture of life that defines the very universe. When you look at Metatron's cube, you'll intuitively feel something alluring about the crisscrossing lines, intersecting circles, and the unique arrangement of each shape. The cube is especially captivating when in 3D, forming a complex geometric structure.

Since you've decided to spiritually connect with the Archangel Metatron, learning about Metatron's cube and how it can help you connect with the revered Archangel is an essential step in the process. Suppose you've already encountered Metatron's cube's beautifully dynamic and complex shape before. In that case, you've probably felt the powerful pull of this hypnotic symbol and wondered what the meaning behind this intricate pattern is. This chapter will help you find that out. Metatron's cube is not just a symbolic shape but has significant spiritual powers that help you connect with the Archangel Metatron more easily. However, to properly harness its power, you must first understand the history and complex dynamics behind this unique shape.

Metatron's Cube and All the Shapes in Creation

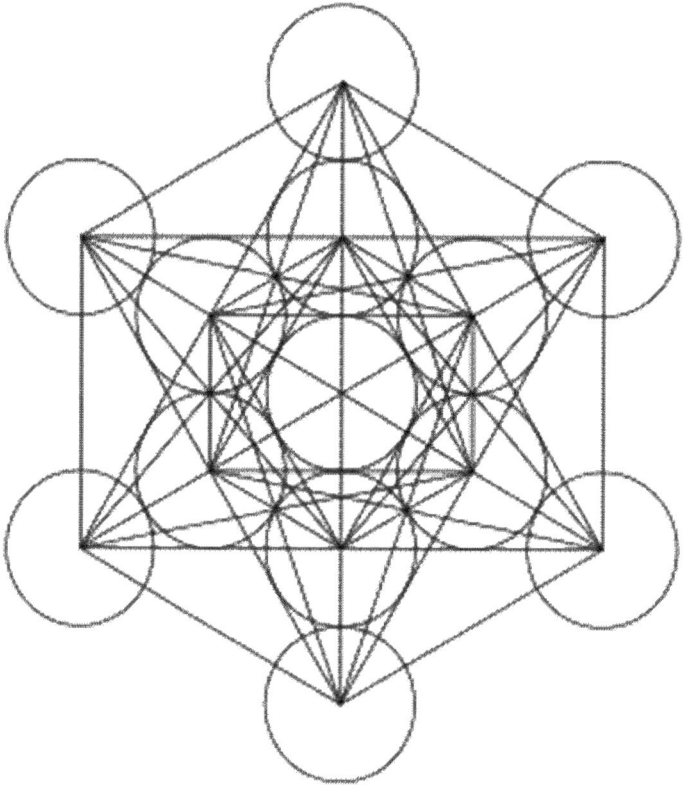

Metatron's cube.
https://commons.wikimedia.org/wiki/File:Metatrons_cube.svg

Why is Metatron's cube so special? After all, it's just a combination of shapes! However, if you focus on the shapes present in this combination, you'll notice that it contains every common shape that exists in the universe! These shapes are considered the building blocks of all physical objects, as they appear throughout creation in everything, whether it's crystals or even human DNA. Do you ever ponder how everything in this universe forms a specific shape and how timeless geometric codes like this cube highlight parallels between patterns in flowers, snowflakes, shells, the corneas of eyes, the DNA molecules that make up our genetic material, and the galaxy itself in which our planet resides? The Creator has designed this world around us, and everything in this world point to the unity and connection of the divine mind that created it.

Various interpretations have been postulated from the symbol of Metatron's cube. Some believe that the cube symbolizes how God has created shapes that fit perfectly together throughout creation and how he designed people's souls and bodies to fit together. The cube represents how this universe's reality is three-dimensional; it has so many aspects and perceptions that things are never one-sided or black and white. Within the cube lies the sphere, so while the cube is said to represent your body, the sphere represents the consciousness of the soul within you.

Meaning and Symbolism of Metatron's Cube

Metatron's cube comprises 13 circles of the same size, with 12 lines extending from the circle at the center towards the other 12 circles. This shape is considered a geometric variant of the Fruit of Life symbol, which is also derived from the Flower of Life symbol. The flower of life symbol is considered to hold all the patterns of creation. Consequently, Metatron's cube symbolizes the birth of the universe and how it infinitely expanded in all directions of time and space. Like the leading theory of how the universe came into existence from a single point, Metatron's cube also begins from a single point in the middle of the shape and then expands outwards.

Everything in our universe is believed to have the same fundamental elements and follow the same principle mathematical laws of physics and nature. Anything and everything in this galaxy, whether it's humans, animals, or plants, is composed of the same materials, albeit in very different ways. And, like many uncovered secrets of this universe, the interwoven patterns and shapes of Metatron's cube have multiple layers that are not easily comprehensible by human minds. However, people have tried interpreting some fundamental concepts from this unique pattern. This can be done by considering the cube's shapes and patterns – not just in 2-dimensions – but also by trying to view it in 3D to further explore it.

Many experts argue that Metatron's cube is just a combination of several sacred patterns like the flower or Fruit of Life. These patterns consist of overlapping circles and make up one unified pattern of creative intelligence. Metatron's cube differs from these patterns because it has 78 additional lines that intersect the 13 circles of the Fruit of Life pattern. This results in a complex pattern consisting of five platonic solids and the Merkabah. The platonic solids are a huge part of Metatron's cube's interpretation and will be discussed later. On the other hand, the Merkabah is a star tetrahedron with eight points, similar in design to the Star of David. This shape is often envisioned as a bright ball of light rotating inside the cube's body.

The Merkabah consists of a downward-facing triangle which symbolizes the descending impulse, and another triangle opposite to it, representing the ascending impulse. The downward shape connects to Earth, whereas the upward triangle connects with the central star of the universe. This is why the Merkabah is sometimes considered a bridge between heaven and earth. The word, *Merkabah*, is roughly translated to "a body of light," which is how it's envisioned. It is said to transport you from this plane to a higher dimension and enhances your spiritual consciousness. When you connect with the archangel Metatron, the Merkabah's creative powers are activated, essentially making you realize your true potential. This will help you transcend your spiritual level and reach a higher level of consciousness.

As for the symbolic representation of Metatron's cube, the unique aligning patterns are said to reflect balance and harmony when viewed from the perspective of sacred geometry. When you look closely at the shapes and patterns adorning the symbol, you'll realize how all the shapes are connected regardless of how small or insignificant they seem. The same is the case with our universe; even small things matter and can significantly alter how things turn out in the big picture. You'll also notice how the circles are connected by lines that reflect the harmony of all things. Some people believe that the circles in Metatron's cube represent the feminine, while the lines are associated with masculine aspects. In other cultures, Metatron's cube is said to attract the guidance and blessings of the Archangel Metatron, as he can attract positive forces and dispel negative energies.

The History Behind Metatron's Cube

Where did the symbol of Metatron's cube come from? As you know by now, the Archangel Metatron has been mentioned in many religious texts, including Kabbalistic, Judaism, and Jewish texts. According to Jewish legends, it's believed that the cube was created from the angel's soul. According to the early scriptures, Metatron created this cube from his soul, meant to oversee the balance and natural floor of the universe. Since the cube is linked to all the shapes existing in the universe, it represents all the patterns that create every single thing in nature. Although the exact dates for its creation are unknown, it is believed to be formed sometime between the creation of this world and 1000 years after. It's more than likely that Metatron's cube has its origins rooted in the symbolic tree of life pattern.

The Theory of Sacred Geometry and Its Origins

Metatron's cube is closely related to the notions of sacred geometry, which have existed for thousands of years in numerous religious teachings. The word "Geometry" comprises two Greek words, "Geos" and "Metron," which refer to "earth" and "measure," respectively. So, geometry refers to the study of shapes and mathematical formulas found in nature. The practice of sacred geometry has roots in old civilizations like the Sumerians, Phoenicians, Greeks, Egyptians, and Minoans. This practice was initially considered sacred and therefore restricted to the priesthood. It was believed by followers of sacred geometry that everything in this world is created according to a specific geometric plan and that studying these natural shapes would uncover great mysteries of the universe.

As you know, Metatron's cube contains all of the geometric shapes and patterns in this world, from circles to spirals, to hexagonal shapes. So, the meaning of Metatron's cube, when viewed from a Sacred Geometry perspective, has many layers, depending on the viewer's understanding. Beginners will observe the cube as a two-dimensional object without focusing on the circles and straight lines and what they represent. On the other hand, experts on this subject will view the cube as three-dimensional and observe the five platonic solids in this sacred shape. Individuals who meditate on the cube as a focal point will begin to see it in five dimensions, revealing new shapes and patterns as it moves through the fourth to the fifth dimension. In some cases, Metatron can divulge heavenly secrets or significant guidance.

So, for the people who are skeptical about the beliefs in sacred geometry, and the power and symbolism of Metatron's cube, it's suggested that they focus a bit harder on this unique shape and try to learn the secrets it hides. Sacred geometry is not some concept formed by over-zealous religious people trying to grasp nothing; it is a real concept that stems from observations, research, and scientific study. This study has resulted in numerous advancements in every field, whether architecture, medicine, music, or art. And not only is sacred geometry real, but it also underpins almost everything humans do and seeks.

The Five Platonic Solids – Five Fundamental Elements of the Universe

Metatron's cube is considered to contain five sacred patterns that connect to the five platonic solids. These shapes make up all the matter in this universe. This concept is named after Plato and connected to his "Theory of Everything." The platonic solids include the tetrahedron, hexahedron, octahedron, dodecahedron, and icosahedron. If you focus on the three-dimensional form of Metatron's cube, you'll notice that two of each pattern are present within the symbol. Each shape is connected to different elementals, like Fire, Earth, Air, Spirit/Ether, and Water. These shapes are the only ones with the same edge length, angle, and face size and perfectly fit in a sphere with all points touching the surface. Forming a perfectly balanced and harmonious pattern, these shapes map everything in this world, from your DNA to the galaxies and beyond. The platonic solids are also called the perfect solids because each of these shapes has perfectly symmetrical sides and formation.

1. Star Tetrahedron – Fire

A star tetrahedron represents the element of fire.
Tomruen, CC BY-SA 4.0 <https://creativecommons.org/licenses/by-sa/4.0>, via Wikimedia Commons: https://commons.wikimedia.org/wiki/File:Stellated_octahedron_stellation_plane.png

The Star Tetrahedron represents the essence of the fire element. It comprises two triangular pyramids and embodies flames' intense and penetrating nature. The precise structure of the shape aligns with the searing heat associated with fire. On the other hand, its symmetrical form symbolizes harmony, balance, stability, and equilibrium.

2. Hexahedron – Earth

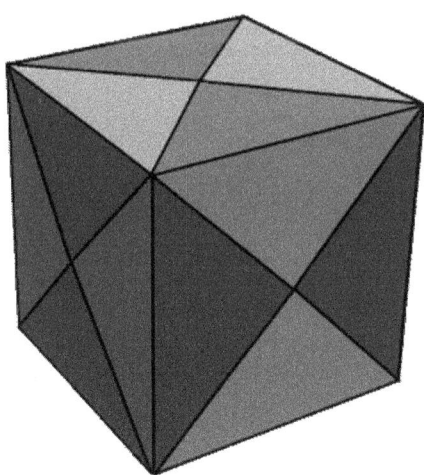

The hexahedron represents the Earth element.
Tomruen, CC BY-SA 4.0 <https://creativecommons.org/licenses/by-sa/4.0>, via Wikimedia Commons: https://commons.wikimedia.org/wiki/File:Tetrakis_hexahedron_cubic.png

The Hexahedron signifies the element of Earth. It resembles a cube and is defined with straight lines embodying the essence of solidity and firmness, which are fundamental attributes of the Earth. The Hexahedron itself rests firmly and evenly on a flat surface, akin to the grounded nature of this planet.

3. Octahedron – Air

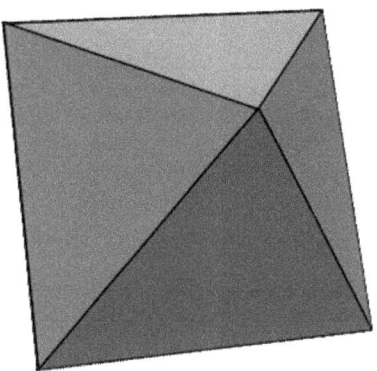

An octahedron represents the element of air.

Tomruen, CC BY-SA 4.0 <https://creativecommons.org/licenses/by-sa/4.0>, via Wikimedia Commons: https://commons.wikimedia.org/wiki/File:Octahedron_orange.png

The Octahedron symbolizes the element of Air. Its sleek form consists of eight equilateral triangles, representing the minute components of air that possess an almost imperceptible smoothness. Just as the Octahedron's structure is composed of seamless triangles, so is the nature of air, which often eludes touch.

4. Icosahedron – Water

The icosahedron is associated with the element of water.

Ancella Simoes from Atlanta, CC BY 2.0 <https://creativecommons.org/licenses/by/2.0>, via Wikimedia Commons: https://commons.wikimedia.org/wiki/File:Origami_Isosahedron_(Design_by_Heinz_Strobl)_(35 95750701).jpg

The Icosahedron is closely associated with the element of Water. Composed of 20 equilateral triangles, it stands as the Platonic Solid with the greatest number of faces. Its harmonious and uniform shape is an apt representation of water, which effortlessly slips away when one attempts to grasp it. The Icosahedron's smooth and flowing structure mirrors water's fluidity and elusive nature.

5. Dodecahedron – Ether

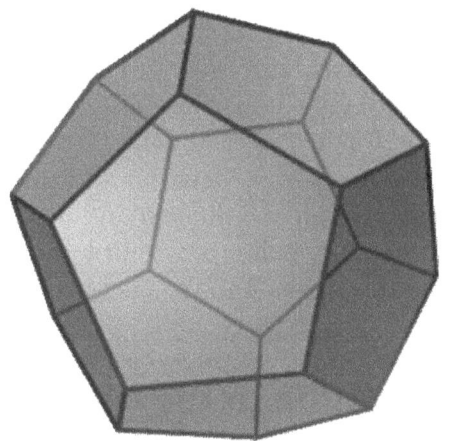

The dodecahedron is associated with the concept of ether.
DTR, CC BY-SA 3.0 <http://creativecommons.org/licenses/by-sa/3.0/>, via Wikimedia Commons: https://commons.wikimedia.org/wiki/File:Dodecahedron.svg

The Dodecahedron is intricately linked to the concept of ether, a distinct element associated with the celestial realm, sky, or space. Ether is often recognized as the fifth essential element that harmoniously combines with the classical elements of fire, earth, air, and water to form the fundamental components of the universe. As a representation of this ethereal element, the Dodecahedron embodies its unique qualities and serves as a symbol connecting the material and spiritual realms.

Connected with the five essential elements that make up this world, the five platonic solids are considered significant to the creation; thus, the cube becomes a symbol of unity and interconnectedness of the world. When you look at Metatron's cube, you'll notice how all the lines, nodes, and circles are connected with one another. Similarly, notice how everything else will be affected if you pull on one string or node from this shape. This is similar to how this world works and how even little things can make a huge difference.

A Tool for Inspiration and Transformation in Sacred Geometry

So, how, when, and where can you use Metatron's cube to help you? Well, for starters, Metatron's cube is known to inspire and motivate humans, whether it's for personal transformation or anything else. According to ancient scholars, studying the sacred patterns and shapes present in the cube and meditating on its patterns will give you inner knowledge of the divine and help with spiritual development. You can use this to further secure your bond with the Archangel Metatron. You can also use this cube for healing and clearing away negative energies. You can call upon the Archangel Metatron and his cube to clear your energy channels whenever you feel drained and demotivated. Archangel Metatron is known for his ability to control the malleability of the physical universe, and this works with the energy of the universe to heal, teach, and purify you.

Metatron's Cube in the Modern Times

The unique symbol of Metatron's cube has inspired numerous masterpieces throughout history in art and architecture. It's even been used as jewelry and meditation practice. Here are some of the most common modern uses of Metatron's cube:

1. **Rituals and Meditation**

Metatron's cube is perfect for use in meditation and other spiritual rituals. It can help with creative blocks and find deeper meaning in life. It also helps promote balance and peace in one's life and ward off negative energies. In some cultures, this symbol is hung on doors and windows to keep evil influences away.

2. **Balancing Energy**

Metatron's cube helps manifest balance and harmony by ensuring that the energy flowing through your body and around you is in proper balance. The symbol can therefore act as a visual focal point that will help you connect with the Archangel Metatron, or it can be used as a concentration tool in meditation, as discussed before. You can place an image of the 2D shape anywhere you like or get a 3D model and put it somewhere in your line of sight.

3. **Fashion and Jewelry**

Metatron's cube enthusiasts often integrate the symbol into their personal style through tattoos and jewelry. This can include necklace pendants, rings, and charms crafted from materials like silver and gold. Additionally, fashion items like t-shirts, jackets, and dresses featuring prints of the symbol are also available. The cube's symmetrical form lends itself to intricate and captivating tattoo designs, making it popular among those seeking complex body art.

4. **Arts and Architecture**

The concept of Metatron's cube is exemplified in the masterpiece Trocto, showcased at the Hyperspace Bypass Construction Zone, an art and design studio in California. This artwork serves as a visual representation of the sacred geometry symbol. Furthermore, the symbol finds its place in the design of various religious structures, from tabernacles and altars to temples, mosques, and churches.

Sacred geometry recognizes Metatron's cube as a symbol containing all the shapes and patterns found within the universe, endowing it with significant potency for rituals and meditations. Its profound meaning has influenced art forms and architectural designs. The inherent power of Metatron's cube is believed to foster balance and facilitate healing. Whether worn as jewelry or carried as a talisman, this powerful symbol attracts positive energy that promotes protection and restoration. Suppose you feel a connection to Metatron's cube and find solace in its symbolism. In that case, it's a good idea to integrate the symbol into your life as a source of inspiration.

Chapter 5: Pillar of Light Meditation

This chapter delves deeper into the ascension process, discussing one of its fundamental elements – the initiation of the Pillar of Light exercise. It will provide further information about this meditation, including its significance and how to receive Metatron's energy by activating it. Besides a few meditation exercises regarding the Pillar of Light activation, you'll also learn a couple of concentration exercises designed to help you focus better.

What Is the Pillar of Light?

The pillar of light is a bridge between your physical body and your higher self.
Derrellwilliams, CC BY-SA 4.0 <https://creativecommons.org/licenses/by-sa/4.0>, via Wikimedia Commons: https://commons.wikimedia.org/wiki/File:Light_pillar_in_winter.jpg

The pillar of light describes a metaphysical bridge between your conscious (present) self and your soul or higher self. You can visualize the pillar of light as a column surrounding your physical body, using it as the center point to connect to your energy and divine empowerment. The width of this pillar around you depends on your energy levels and ability to manifest it. The more energy you can channel into manifesting the column of light, the stronger it will become, allowing great sources of spiritual light to come into your life. It will also enable you to receive and send spiritual messages when building a connection with your higher self and the divine.

A pillar of light is an ideal communication tool between your physical and metaphysical aspects – which is where Metatron's help comes in handy. He can guide you through the journey of activating the pillar of light and receiving more guidance, wisdom, and inspiration for elevating your spirituality. He can also teach you how to use the pillar of light to enhance your psychic abilities.

The concept of the pillar relies on a connection to the divine consciousness. The column extends from way above your head into the heavenly realm and under your feet into the ground. Energy from both sources can move through it, nurturing your own energies. Once the pillar is activated, it dispels all the lower frequencies, enabling you to further raise your vibrations and reach spiritual enlightenment. You can never establish a meaningful connection to your higher self without a pillar of light. The column acts as a reminder of your spiritual sovereignty – reintroducing your divine nature and activating a deep consciousness.

Fully activating your pillar of light takes a lot of energy and practice. You'll need to channel a lot of light and high-vibrational energy into your energetic body. You must empower your chakras with cleansing energy so they can enable you to radiate your energy toward the higher bodies. However, each time you do this, you are rendering your pillar more powerful until it becomes so potent that you won't need to consciously focus on activating it. Remember that your intention matters the most – as with any other spiritual work. If you truly want to activate your pillar of light, you must channel your energy into manifesting it.

Activating the Pillar of Light

You can do this meditation at any time of the day, which makes it great for those who haven't yet established a schedule for spiritual exercises. That said, finding a regular slot for it is a good idea. This will improve your focus and bring you closer to your goal of spiritual alignment and ascension.

Instructions:

1. The activity is designed to ground and connect you with the Earth and the universe, so it's best done as a standing exercise. Standing makes you plant your feet firmly on the ground. Relax your shoulders just enough to avoid being distracted by uncomfortable sensations in your body.
2. Close your eyes and focus on something that brings you joy. Smile, and let this smile melt the stress around you – see it drip onto the ground.
3. Imagine your feet sinking into the ground, extending roots that travel into the earth like plant roots seeking nourishment. Feel the roots moving out in all directions, north, south, east, and west, above and below. They connect you to the energy of the universe and divine essence.
4. Feel your energy infuse with the energy harnessed by your roots. Suddenly, a source of light comes up from the ground, travels up the back of your legs, up your spine, and flows into your heart and head.
5. Feel how the energy begins to vibrate inside you, the light illuminating you from the inside out. When you feel that the energy can no longer be continued inside you, imagine it being divided into two powerful streams.
6. Imagine the streams flowing down your arms and radiating out of your palms, surrounding you with golden light. The light infuses your energy with the energy of the earth.
7. Imagine being connected to the divine and the earth simultaneously. You're now a bridge between the heavenly realm and the human one. As you focus on this awareness, you feel your every tissue and cell becoming saturated with the bright light that unites the energy of nature and divine empowerment.

8. Your entire being vibrates with bright light and becomes lighter and lighter. You become aware of your divine energy and let it expand toward the universe.
9. As you let the bright light course through your body, your divine energy becomes rooted in your consciousness.
10. Call on your spiritual guides (including Archangel Metatron) and ask them to help you use the light for a higher good. Ask them to help you bring love and spiritual fulfillment to yourself and others, and thank them for their assistance.
11. Complete the meditation by letting the image of your spiritual allies and the light go. Gently bring awareness back to the present as you open your eyes and let your mind be filled with mundane thoughts.

Short Pillar of Light Activation Practice

Here is an easy-to-do exercise to activate the pillar of light and initiate your ascension journey. While this might not allow you to fully open the pillar right away, with time and practice, you'll be able to do it with just a few simple breaths. In the meantime, this short exercise will help you start mastering the basic steps.

Instructions:
1. Find a comfortable position and relax by taking a few deep breaths. Keep your feet on the ground – preferably do this exercise outside (where you can be closer to nature).
2. Imagine positive energy traveling down the center of your body, leaving you smiling and stress-free.
3. Visualize your feet being grounded into the earth, uniting you with it, like ice melting into water. You can almost feel your feet being absorbed into the soil beneath them.
4. Feel your energy extending into the ground, like a tree growing its roots. Imagine your roots traveling all the way into the core of the planet. See your core connection to your roots but also to a powerful source of light suddenly surrounding you.
5. The light fills you with empowering energy. It travels into your body, down your arms, and fills the space around you with golden light.

6. Imagine yourself being completely saturated by this light. As you inhale, the energy expands your body and the surrounding space. As you exhale, the energy wraps around you like a cocoon.
7. You feel weightless, almost as if you are floating in the heavenly realm. You can feel the clouds around your waist – yet your feet are still connected to the earth.
8. You're now a pillar of light. As you inhale, imagine overflowing your being with bright light, your center becoming illuminated by this light.
9. You're now connected to your divine being – a being of pure consciousness. Now say the following invocation:

    "I am who I am.

    I am now calling upon the presence of the divine,

    I am now calling upon the presence of Archangel Metatron.

    I am surrounding my ego.

    May the divine will become my will."

10. If needed, repeat the invocation twice more. This will help you channel stronger focus and deeper your connection to your spiritual self.
11. Now, you are free of anything that no longer serves you and empowered with your pillar of light – the divine source that will prompt your ascension. Rest in this awareness for as long as you need to, then slowly let your thoughts flow back into your mind.

Pillar of Light Activation Meditation

The following practice will help you experience the activation of light within. It's an exercise that focuses on breathing and improving contention to manifest your desire to activate and channel the energy of your divine light. The meditation will become your source of peace and reminder of your love for your divine existence.

Instructions:

1. Find a comfortable position – sitting or lying down.
2. Take a few deep breaths, and allow your eyes to close naturally. As you feel yourself relaxing, become aware of the sensations near your spine. Imagine a bright energy source emerging from your spine, pulling you upwards.

3. Connect with your breath consciously, beginning with a simple awareness of your breathing. As you breathe in, notice the energy that enters your body.
4. With each breath you take, feel your heart expand, and the energy revitalizes your soul.
5. Repeat the simple "Ahhh" mantra six times. With each repetition, feel the energy vibrating through your body. Continue taking deep, conscious breaths.
6. With each breath, allow your awareness to move toward your heart. Relax and connect to your soul, deeper and deeper.
7. Welcoming your breath, aligning yourself with your awareness of every part of your body until it reaches the top of your head. When it does, allow it to open your crown, welcoming a bright light into it.
8. See this bright light shining upon you, penetrating your head and expanding your inner light. Welcome the light with your heart and every cell of your body. Feel how it fills your cells.
9. Your heart is filled with joy as you see the light slowly seeping outside, embracing your body just as it did with your insides.
10. Imagine this bright light creating a column of light, centering you in the middle of itself. With each breath you take, the column radiates brighter and fills you with more empowering energy.
11. Allow yourself to experience the power of the pillar of light you're in this moment. You can affirm it to yourself by saying:

    "I am a pillar of light."
12. You can start empowering this pillar even more with deep breathwork. Place your thumbs over the nail of your index fingers. The other fingers should be outstretched as your hands rest relaxed on your knees, palms up.
13. Find a steady rhythm for your breath. The goal is to contract your abdomen as you breathe out through your nose while your inhalations remain natural. Speed up your breathing while maintaining the same pattern for 10-15 seconds.
14. Then breathe as fast as you can for about 5 seconds, and feel empowered by the pillar of light.

15. Take a deep breath and hold it for a few seconds. Feel the activation within you. Exhale gently and keep your body still and relaxed.
16. Focus on extending your inner experience. If any thoughts come, allow them to drift in and out and bring your awareness back to your breath, reestablishing the powerful stillness within.
17. Take a gentle deep breath, and be aware of the pillar of light - penetrating and surrounding you. Feel your heart filling with gratitude for this light and the empowerment of your mind, body, and soul.
18. As you breathe in again, bring your awareness to the space around you. Slowly stretch your body as you open your eyes and let your everyday thoughts return.

Improving Your Focus

When trying to master the pillar of light meditation, beginners often have trouble focusing on their intention. Whether due to a lack of experience or because they're overwhelmed by the sudden energy shift in them, some people have trouble concentrating long enough to manifest long-term changes. If you have similar issues, you'll be happy to learn that improving your focus simply takes a little practice. If you can take a few minutes a day to pause your thoughts and quiet your mind, you'll soon discover the strength you need to channel your focus in the right direction. Consider practicing improving your focus as an opportunity to be more present with yourself. It helps raise awareness of what you want to create in your life and what no longer resonates with this goal. It also teaches you that you can take control of your thoughts and actions and use them to connect with spiritual helpers like Metatron and initiate your spiritual growth. This affirmation-based mediation allows you to connect to your inner self. Learning to ground yourself can improve your focus and reaffirm your intention of creating the pillar of light.

Instructions:
1. Start by taking several deep breaths. While you do, focus on an intention of aligning with your divine self.
2. Empty your mind of all thoughts except for your intent. If it wanders in any other direction, shift your focus back to your intention. If you're having difficulties concentrating, focus on the

sensations in your body.
3. Call on Archangel Metatron (and any other spiritual guide) to join you and empower you as you take control of your focus.
4. Imagine a ball of light descending from up in the sky, traveling toward you. As it descends, it leaves a trail of bright light behind it – forming a pillar that connects it to the center of the universe.
5. Suddenly, the ball of light stops just above your head. Then it descends further into your crown and travels down to your toes, filling your entire body with light.
6. Feel how your body radiates with light – as an extension of the magnificent pillar of light above you. The pillar of light shines through you and from you. It's filling you with divine power, unconditional love, and the angelic essence of Archangel Metatron.
7. Focus on your breathing, sensing how you are refilled with the angel's energy with each breath. Tap into this energy and use it to boost your vibes and fuel your intention of connecting to your divine self.
8. Your goal is to take control of your divine energy – so you can radiate it toward others. Feel free to keep focusing on this target until you feel that your frequencies are starting to align with the divine frequency. The pillar of light will raise your frequencies so you can accomplish this.
9. As you sit, proclaim these words:

   "I accept myself as I am.

   I am an aspect of the Creator.

   I align every aspect of my being to this truth.

   I know who I am.

   I know what I am.

   I know who my allies are."
10. After each line, stop to take a deep breath and channel your energy toward your intention. Tap into the part of you who knows who you are in a spiritual sense.
11. Sit quietly under the pillar of energy for a few moments. When you feel it's time, slowly return to your thoughts. Enjoy being empowered by the pillar of light and the knowledge of being able

to focus on any goal you establish for yourself.

Opening Your Heart

Opening up your heart is another fundamental step in any spiritual work. Whether you want to connect with Metatron or other spiritual guides or facilitate your ascension, you must be open to accepting their energies. The following pillar of light exercise helps activate your true potential by opening your heart and filling it with positive emotions. This enables you to cultivate love, compassion, and sincerity that fills your soul, allowing it to become enlightened and connected to the pillar of light. You can do this as a standalone exercise or perform it before a deeper meditation. Whichever way you use it, remember to practice daily for at least a month before taking a pause. It only takes 5-10 minutes a day. When the month is over, you'll have a much stronger connection to Archangel Metatron and the divine. It might take you longer in the beginning, but once you master it, it will go much faster.

Instructions:

1. Start in a relaxed standing position. If you haven't performed similar meditations before and have trouble relaxing, do the exercise in a sitting position a couple of times. After a few seated sessions, you can switch to the standing version.

2. As you relax, let your body slowly settle. You might have a subconscious urge to move any parts of your body. This is entirely natural – let your body make any movements it needs to make. It will help reinforce the thought that you're free to do whatever feels comfortable.

3. When you feel relaxed, take a deep breath and imagine a light entering your head.

4. As you do, place your hands in front of your heart in a prayer position. Invite the light to cleanse your ego, starting with your trusting heart and soul.

5. Move your hands toward your sides, lifting your palms toward the sky, in honor of all the spirits and creations in the universe, including Archangel Metatron.

6. As you feel your heart being opened, lift your hands and slowly place them on your head. Imagine your mind being transformed due to all the positivity emanating from your heart and soul.

7. Remove your hands from your head and start lowering them, using them to outline the contours of your body. Focus on channeling the energies that transformed your heart and mind across your entire body, healing it from the inside out.
8. As your body starts to heal, you will feel more connected to the universe and grounded in nature. Repeat the hand movements from step 4 twice more.
9. With your first repetition, focus on aligning your energy with the lights and channeling it toward the space around you. The goal is to cleanse your sacred space and dispel any energy that could close your heart and mind.
10. The second repetition is to extend your newly empowered energies further, creating deeper bonds with the universe and Archangel Metatron.
11. You've opened your heart and activated the pillar of light. You are ready to take the next step toward full activation and delve deeper into your spiritual practice.

Chapter 6: Angelic Reiki and Healing

If you yearn for a deeper connection with the angelic realm, you must always look for different ways to help you connect with the angels. As it turns out, you can connect spiritually with the angelic realm in countless ways. It's almost as if the heavens have opened up and bestowed inspiration, spurred you into action, and implored you to ask for help, guidance, or direction in your life. Among these divine beings, one Archangel has been more gracious than any others and has extended his hand to humans, inviting them to find inspiration, creativity, and profound guidance. Metatron is more receptive to you than any other Archangel you'll encounter.

In the previous chapter, you learned about the transformative power of the pillar of light meditation and how you can use this technique to connect with Archangel Metatron. You tapped into the depths of your soul and tried to unravel the mysteries of the universe or of your own life. Now, it's time to embrace another facet of spiritual connection, one that complements meditation just like two sides of a coin. Reiki is a metamorphic technique that helps you harness the mystical energy flowing through the cosmos to channel it for healing and spiritually opening yourself. Much like meditation, Reiki allows you to tap into the divine frequencies that resonate within and around us. In simple terms, it helps you spiritually connect with angelic beings, such as Metatron.

In this chapter, you'll learn what Reiki is all about and how you can use it to connect with Archangel Metatron. Through this practice, you can open your heart and mind to his divine presence and immerse yourself in a reality where energies and intentions intermingle, and healing seamlessly merges with enlightenment. But that's not all you'll learn. Once you master Reiki symbols and their traditional practice, this chapter will dive into angelic Reiki, which is more centered on connecting with angels, particularly the Archangel Metatron. So, prepare yourself to witness the healing magic of a Reiki session, and get ready to form a transcendent bond with Metatron.

The Basics of Reiki

Reiki therapy is a method of guiding energy throughout the body to encourage healing and mindfulness. The Reiki belief system explains that the practice itself doesn't produce energy or heal anything on its own. Instead, it's a channel for energy, similar to how a garden hose acts as a channel for water. Reiki's roots can be traced back to early 20th century Japan, and this method is defined as a form of energy healing. It is based on the concept that everyone has an invisible life force energy flowing through their bodies at all times. In fact, it's believed that everything in this world comprises energy and is surrounded by energy. By encouraging a healthy flow of this energy through your body, Reiki can work wonders for your spiritual health. This technique is perfect for stress reduction and relaxation but also promotes healing. The principle behind the concept of Reiki is that if a person's life force energy is depleted, imbalanced, or weakened, then they're more likely to get sick or feel stressed, and when it's high and flows freely, they're more capable of being healthy and happy.

This method is considered to be mainly a spiritual practice but is not limited to any religion. The word Reiki itself is composed of two Japanese words, "*Rei*" and "*Ki*," which mean "God's wisdom" and "Life force energy," respectively. So, Reiki actually translates to spiritually guided life force energy. During a Reiki treatment, you'll feel a glowing radiance around you, which will treat not just your body but also your mind, emotions, and spirit. Numerous health benefits come with the practice of Reiki, and although it doesn't necessarily cure diseases, it does promote healing of all kinds, both physical and spiritual. Reiki is usually practiced by a professional Reiki therapist who has done extensive training and acquired the proper knowledge to practice this art form.

Traditionally, Reiki is taught by the sensei (teacher) to their students through attunement, which is basically an initiation ceremony that helps open up the student's energy channels to help improve the flow of energy. Once these channels have been opened, they remain accessible to the practitioner for the rest of their life. Just like meditation, Reiki is also considered a spiritual practice. It is taught at three levels, where practitioners on the first level practice this technique on themselves or others through light touch. Then at the second level, practitioners learn the ability to perform it at a distance, and third-degree or master practitioners are capable of teaching and initiating other people into Reiki.

How It Works

Many people ask, "How exactly does Reiki work?" Well, there's no single answer to this. Most practitioners and Reiki researchers don't have an explanation for the mechanism of action associated with Reiki. However, several theories, though not concrete, provide a rough idea of how this method takes place. One popular theory, which addresses the science behind this process, explains a phenomenon known as the "biofield," which is basically an electromagnetic field that permeates and surrounds every living organism.

Experts say this electromagnetic field extends 15 feet or more from the human body. In fact, there is evidence of energy being present within and around your body all around us. For instance, the heart produces an electric field observed through an ECG, while the brain also produces an electric field, albeit at a much lower level than the heart. All of the body's cells are known to produce positive and negative electric charges, which result in magnetic fields.

So, according to this theory, when Reiki is performed, and the energies of the magnetic fields of two human beings interact, these energies are altered or influenced, you could say. It's believed that the biofield that surrounds every person is what guides their bodily functions. Reiki energy is said to influence said biofield, thus affecting a person's physical and spiritual energy. So, in essence, the practice of this technique gathers and directs the biofield energy to you through thoughts, intentions, and touch.

Some Reiki Techniques

Similar to meditation, there are so many types of Reiki techniques and modalities developed that it becomes difficult to learn and remember all of them. Whether it's for centering purposes, clearing away negative energies, beaming energy, extracting harmful energies, infusing energies, or smoothing and raking the aura, Reiki takes on many forms. Reiki practitioners often use crystals and healing wands to enhance the quality of their practice. However, in essence, Reiki does not rely on any instruments other than the practitioner. A general Reiki session lasts about an hour, and the number of times you take a session depends on your goals. Similarly, the type of Reiki practice you want to perform is also up to you. Some common techniques include:

- **Usui Reiki:** The original form of Reiki, which originated in Japan. This technique involves physical touch to channel the healing energy throughout one's body. It helps promote emotional, spiritual, and physical health.
- **Karuna Reiki:** This technique is comparatively more complex than the traditionally practiced Reiki. It incorporates some additional symbols and movements to address the psychological and emotional aspects of healing. You should practice this method when you're looking to focus on compassion and deep healing.
- **Kundalini Reiki:** This powerful type of Reiki is perfect for spiritual growth and healing, which is what you'll prefer when trying to connect with an Archangel. The Kundalini event is located at the base of the spine, and this technique targets that area to harness this special healing energy.
- **Shamanic Reiki**: This method incorporates shamanic practices into Reiki techniques. The many indigenous spiritual traditions, like connecting with spirit guides or forces of nature, can come in especially handy when you're learning to work with an Archangel.
- **Crystal Reiki**: This technique involves using crystals and gemstones to speed up the healing process, whether spiritual or physical. For this, crystals are placed on or near the body during the reiki session.

- **Tibetan Reiki:** As you can tell from the name, this Reiki technique combines the teachings and methods of Tibetan Buddhism. This includes using mantras, sacred symbols, and rituals to help with the healing process and spiritual transformation.
- **Angelic Reiki:** Angelic Reiki, which will be the focus of this chapter, helps you work with angelic beings and their healing energies. For this, you need to connect with angelic guides to channel their healing energies and guidance.
- **Seichim Reiki:** Seichim Reiki, also called Sekhem or SKHM, is a little-known Egyptian form of Reiki that includes balancing masculine and feminine energy. This method provides deep healing and self-awareness.

Each type and modality offers a unique perspective and can be used for specific purposes. It's best to stick to general and angelic Reiki practices for this journey. Make sure these techniques resonate with you and meet your specific needs.

Reiki Symbols and Their Meanings

The founder of traditional Reiki, Mikao Usui, introduced several symbols to this powerful technique. These symbols are known to be calming and spiritual and have specific meanings that decide when they should be used. What are these symbols used for, you wonder? During Reiki treatments, of course! The practitioner draws these symbols on the receiver's hands, eyes, or in the air. During Reiki training, these symbols are taught and have to be memorized, and are also used during attunement ceremonies. There are four main symbols in designated orders, with a few additional symbols in other Reiki systems. These include:

1. Cho Ku Rei

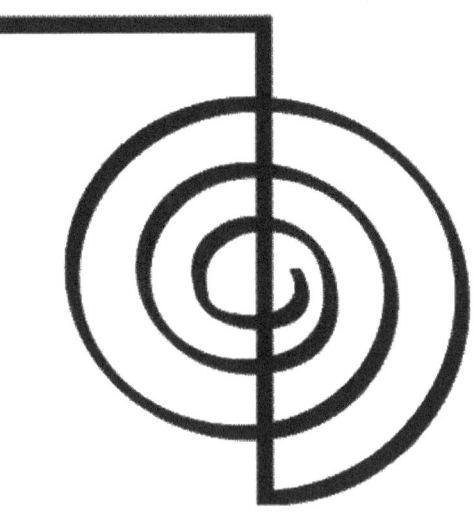

Reiki power symbol.
https://commons.wikimedia.org/wiki/File:Cho-Ku-Rei_(Reiki_Symbol).svg

The top symbol in the Usui Reiki system is the Cho Ku Rei, the power symbol. This symbol helps turn on the switch of the energy flow, drawing the life force power from the upper chakra, going all the way through all seven chakras. It translates to "focusing the energy of the universe here."

2. Sei Hei Ki

Reiki symbol of harmony.
Stephen Buck The Reiki Sangha, CC BY-SA 4.0 <https://creativecommons.org/licenses/by-sa/4.0>, via Wikimedia Commons: https://commons.wikimedia.org/wiki/File:Seiheiki.jpg

The next Reiki symbol is the Sei Hei Ki, considered the harmony symbol. This symbol roughly translates to "Earth and Sky Meet," highlighting the harmony between the heavenly and earthly energy forces. From its drawing pattern, you can observe that it's also about harmony between the mental and emotional energy and the creativity on the right side of the brain versus the logic on the left side.

3. Hon Sha Ze Sho Nen

Distance healing symbol.
Stephen Buck The Reiki Sangha, CC BY-SA 4.0 <https://creativecommons.org/licenses/by-sa/4.0>, via Wikimedia Commons: https://commons.wikimedia.org/wiki/File:Honshazeshonen.jpg

This symbol is considered the most complex and challenging one to draw out of all the Reiki symbols. The Distance Healing symbol translates to "Across past, present, and future." This symbol empowers Reiki healing across these elements of time and space. For instance, this symbol can be used to perform Reiki to help those not in the same space or even in the same time period.

4. **Dai Ko Myo**

Great shining light symbol.
Stephen Buck The Reiki Sangha, CC BY-SA 4.0 <https://creativecommons.org/licenses/by-sa/4.0>, via Wikimedia Commons: https://commons.wikimedia.org/wiki/File:Daikomyo.jpg

This is the last of the four main Usui Reiki symbols and is considered to be the Master Symbol. This symbol translates to "The Great Shining Light" because this symbol is all about connecting with the universe's life force energy beyond the restrictions of this world. This symbol is learned in level three or master-level training of Reiki and is considered very sacred to the Reiki system.

5. **Raku Symbol**

Completion symbol.
Juan Camilo Guerrero, CC BY-SA 4.0 <https://creativecommons.org/licenses/by-sa/4.0>, via Wikimedia Commons: https://commons.wikimedia.org/wiki/File:Raku_Symbol.jpg

The Raku symbol is considered to be the completion or grounding symbol, which helps conclude a session by channeling the energy from the crown to the root of the body. This symbol also helps draw a clear separation between the practitioner and the receiver. Although not part of the four main Reiki symbols, this symbol is considered just as important. It resembles a lightning bolt and is often called the "Fire Serpent."

Angelic Reiki: Enhancing Connection with Metatron

Angelic Reiki is a lot like traditional Reiki in many ways, but it also has significant differences that make the process more specific to its intended purposes. Angelic Reiki is a tranquil and powerful healing modality that works at a soul level and helps you channel guidance from the Angels. Through this technique, you can treat the root causes of any condition and bring about healing and balance in your life. This system of Reiki helps you connect intimately with the angels as they move through you and bring in harmony and guidance from the divine. As you know, all forms of Reiki healing include hand movements that channel the life force energy through the recipient. But where this energy comes from depends on the type of energy healing being practiced. In the case of Angelic Reiki, the abundance of energy is channeled from the angels, specifically, the Archangel Metatron.

What does an Angelic Reiki healing session feel like?

An Angelic Reiki session, much like any traditional Reiki treatment session, should be carried out in calm, tranquil, and dimly lit environments. To practice this technique, find a place where you're comfortable, away from the noise, and where you feel peaceful. Once you're in a nice, relaxed position, close your eyes, and get the Reiki session started. For this, you can either learn all the Angelic Reiki techniques by yourself or get the help of a professional Reiki practitioner. You will feel very deep feelings and physical sensations during an Angelic Reiki session. People have reported feeling:

- Tingling
- Warmth
- Shivering
- Numbness

- Coolness

Benefits of Angelic Reiki

If you've never practiced Angelic Reiki or just Reiki of any kind, you've been missing out on so many benefits. This practice is spiritually healing for you and will strengthen your bond with whatever angel you're trying to connect with. Archangel Metatron is one of the most accessible and helpful Archangels out of all. He will surely help you with any problems you're facing and guide you in the right direction. Some benefits of Angelic Reiki include:

- Enhanced self-healing
- Improved sleep quality
- Pain relief
- Restores chakra balance
- Improved energy levels
- Stress reduction
- Enhanced immune system
- Strengthens intuition and spiritual development
- Eliminates negative energy

What is the difference between Angelic Reiki and Usui Reiki?

In some ways, Usui Reiki, or traditional Reiki practice, is similar to Angelic Reiki, but not exactly the same. Although all systems of Reiki fundamentally have the same purpose, which is providing powerful healing of one's life force energy, Angelic Reiki has significant differences from Usui Reiki, which can include:

1. **Source of Energy**

In traditional Reiki practice, the energy is manifested and sustained by the practitioner and then channeled through the receiver's body. On the other hand, in Angelic Reiki practice, the energy is purely divine, channeled by the practitioner, and transmitted to the recipient through touch or with sacred symbols.

2. **Attunements**

During the attunement process, the energy channels are opened by the Reiki Master teacher for traditional Reiki practices. However, for Angelic Reiki, the attunement is done by a specific healing angel assigned to every person. In this case, it should be Metatron who should be called upon for the attunement process.

3. Practitioner's Role

The practitioner's role is considered pretty significant in traditional Reiki practices, as they're responsible for using their intuition and healing abilities to find the areas of the body that need to heal most. On the other hand, Angelic Reiki does not require a practitioner to have an active role in the healing session and only acts as a passive vessel while letting the angel's guidance direct them throughout the process.

Angelic Reiki Healing Session

An Angelic Reiki session will heal spiritually and help you feel connected more closely with the Archangel Metatron. You'll feel the gentle and loving energies of the Archangel and feel at ease by the end of the session. Sticking with a healer is best unless you have proper training in performing a Reiki session. The healer will act as a conduit for the angelic healing energy and play a crucial role in the whole process. Here's a step-by-step explanation of how the process will take place:

- **Preparation:** To prepare for the Reiki session, the practitioner cleanses the room, lights candles, and places crystals near the treatment table or chair. Sometimes, soft music is also preferred.
- **Invocation:** Next, a connection needs to be formed with the Archangel Metatron, which is done by invoking the angel's presence and asking for his guidance. The practitioner usually does this with a silent prayer or a verbal intention.
- **Energy Scanning:** The healer/practitioner then uses their sensitivity, intuition, and psychic abilities to scan the recipient's aura and chakras. They may do this by moving their hands over the recipient's body or through their clairvoyant abilities.
- **Energy Clearing:** The healer then uses the Reiki symbols, the four main ones, and other additional symbols desired to clear the recipient's energy blockages, negative patterns, or stagnant energy.
- **Healing Intuition:** Then the main process of Reiki starts when the healer uses their hands to channel the angelic energy through the recipient's chakras. During the session, the practitioner receives guidance from Metatron and inspires them

to perform this technique perfectly.
- **Chakra Alignment:** Next, the practitioner focuses on balancing and aligning the chakras. This is done by removing any blockages from their chakra points and restoring the free flow of energy.
- **Closing and Grounding:** Towards the end of the session, the healer gradually reduces the flow of healing energy. They guide the recipient into a grounded state, ensuring that the client feels centered, present, and fully integrated with the healing energies they received.

The presence of Metatron in Angelic Reiki amplifies its transformative essence. The healer's profound connection with Metatron's energy infuses the healing session with divine light. Through this connection, messages and insights flow, offering profound healing and guidance. One's chakras align and harmonize, which helps restore balance and vitality to the body. Within this sacred modality, miracles await those who open their hearts to the boundless possibilities of divine love and healing.

Chapter 7: Crystals to Connect with Metatron

As you know by now, angels are essentially beings made of energy, the celestial messengers between mankind and the divine. The Archangels are no exception to this but are significantly distinguishable from other angels. Each archangel has specific crystals and gemstones which resonate with their abilities, energies, and attributes. After all, crystals are composed of the earth's energy and act as conductors or amplifiers. Therefore, they are perfect tools to help you communicate, heal, and become more in tune with the angelic realm. Crystals and gemstones have an invisible frequency that resonates with the energy frequency of specific angels, or in this case, Archangels.

Many consider crystals to be energy stores that enhance spiritual processes like healing, guiding, protecting, grounding, etc. Archangel crystals can be used to absorb the heavenly energy of Archangels and anchor this energy to the earth and you. Of course, working with crystals isn't something mandatory when working with Archangels. However, these crystals improve the whole process of connecting with Archangels significantly, especially Archangel Metatron, who has certain crystals that can encompass his creative guidance perfectly. This chapter will guide you in using crystals when connecting with the Archangel Metatron. You'll learn about using crystals in spiritual processes and connecting with the divine.

The Basics of Crystal Healing

You'll often encounter healing crystals in many spiritual circles because of their apparent magical, metaphysical, and energetically healing properties. In fact, numerous theories explain how crystals can enhance a spiritual process or merely have a placebo effect. One of the most common explanations is that crystals have certain vibrational frequencies aligned with specific outcomes or tangible results in real life.

When you have certain crystals around you whose vibrational frequencies align with your body, soul, or goals, you'll feel an invisible force helping you every step of the way, whether with spiritual healing, angelic communication, or to get divine guidance. And even if you're still skeptical about the efficacy of healing crystals, even if there is no concrete fact proving their properties, they can still play a deeply supportive role in your spirituality and help improve your intuition.

Crystals are associated with certain outcomes like healing, love, protection, clarity, and cleansing, any of which you could be seeking when trying to connect with the archangel Metatron. Plus, crystals can serve as a physical reminder of an intention you're keeping or a goal you're striving towards. For example, you may keep a crystal associated with clarity on your work desk. Even if you don't truly believe in its metaphysical powers, you'll be reminded of your intention whenever you look at it, and automatically work better. Or maybe, you wear a rose quartz necklace to remind yourself to be loving and empathetic to the people around you. Now, whenever you gain sight of this crystal, you'll naturally be more conscious of your behavior with others, try to make it better, and be more compassionate.

Crystals can also help you feel grounded and centered. In this day and age, it's easy to feel scattered and believe you're a mess. Almost everyone gets this feeling of being lost and dissociated because of the sheer number of responsibilities and tasks they have every day. This is where crystal meditation comes in. Certain crystals promote peace, calmness, and serenity and can help bring you back to the center. Finally, crystals are also commonly used for rituals, incantations, and manifestations. They are a popular tool used to try to connect with the divine, especially the Archangels. In fact, almost every Archangel has several crystals they favor.

Benefits of Healing Crystals

The use of healing crystals isn't something that has gained popularity in this century but has been in practice for thousands of years. Back in Egyptian times, these beautiful minerals were used to cleanse and protect against evil spirits. Today, crystals are used for various purposes and have several benefits, some proven by facts, while others are reinforced by experience. These include:

1. **Placebo Effect**

The placebo effect is the most identifiable result of the effectiveness of using crystals for healing. It is a phenomenon in which people feel a significant improvement in their symptoms after receiving a treatment with little to no therapeutic value. In this case, the placebo effect results from using healing crystals to speed up regular healing processes. It doesn't matter if crystals do, in fact, help the process; a person's belief in this method of treatment is enough to make a difference.

2. **Emotional and Physical Healing**

Emotional imbalances are common, but did you know you can alleviate these mental pressures and emotional worries with specific crystals? Since crystals are known to carry unique energy, they can help target emotional stresses and help relieve some stress from your mind. On the flip side, these rocks and gemstones are also known for aiding physical healing and providing pain relief. For instance, amethyst can be used to relieve pain, while hematite can be used to improve blood circulation and grounding.

3. **Cross-Cultural Significance**

Crystal healing has a rich history and an undeniable cultural significance attached to it. This method has been utilized for centuries, whether in traditional medicine or spiritual development; it holds prominence in many cultures. So, even though there are not a lot of scientific facts proving the effectiveness of crystals, their historical prominence should count for something.

4. **The Piezoelectric Effect**

Suppose you're familiar with the basics of electronics. In that case, you'd know that the piezoelectric effect can also be used to explain vibrational medicine. However, it is mainly used to describe the generation of electricity. This effect basically enables crystals to convert mechanical force into another form of energy like sound, electricity, or light and then amplify it. When this concept is applied to crystal healing, this effect magnifies the energy flow in a person's body or surroundings.

5. Spiritual Communication

Since crystals can amplify and transmit energy, they're commonly used for spiritual communication and to get guidance. Particular crystals have the vibrational frequency to enhance a person's intuition and psychic abilities and help them access higher states of consciousness. They can also be used to balance and align energy chakras in the body. Specific crystals are associated with each chakra and can be used to remove energy blockages and improve energy flow.

The Most Popular Crystals

In the world of spiritual communication, and angelic guidance, there is a vast array of crystals and gemstones that act as powerful energy conduits to help connect with the celestial beings. From the shimmering quartz crystals to the vibrant amethyst and the mysterious obsidian, there's no shortage of crystals to help you commune with the divine. The most popular ones include:

1. Amethyst

Amethyst can quell anxiety.
https://unsplash.com/photos/jLWLxX6i3R8?utm_source=unsplash&utm_medium=referral&utm_content=creditShareLink

Amethyst is one of the most popular crystals – and for a good reason. In addition to its vibrant purple hue, and beautiful design, it can quell anxiety and even improve one's sleep quality. Amethyst is said to target the crown chakra, which is located at the top of the head, resulting in a feeling of peace and tranquility for your brain. Although not proven, amethysts are known for their ability to ease headaches and migraines and strengthen intuition. Many people believe that placing an amethyst crystal by your bedside can calm your mind and bring you pleasant dreams.

2. Rose Quartz

Rose quartz is associated with love.
https://unsplash.com/photos/WKkTwwBILec?utm_source=unsplash&utm_medium=referral&utm_content=creditShareLink

Like its pinkish color, Rose quartz is associated with love and relationships. This crystal is wonderful to keep around if you manifest love or want a new relationship. It can also be useful if you're already on an emotional rollercoaster and don't know how to solve your problems. Rose quartz crystals are known to bring empathy, reconciliation, kindness, and love to those around them. If not needed for any of the reasons above, pink quartz can help bring you a feeling of peace, which is a good enough reason to keep it around.

3. Black Tourmaline

Black tourmaline absorbs negative energy.
Rama, CC BY-SA 3.0 FR <https://creativecommons.org/licenses/by-sa/3.0/fr/deed.en>, via Wikimedia Commons: https://commons.wikimedia.org/wiki/File:Tourmaline-MCG_79448-P4150859-black.jpg

The black tourmaline targets the root chakra, which is located at the center of the body. This absorbent crystal can soak up all the negative energies that approach you or are already in your life. This is a grounding crystal that can also be used in many spiritual rituals.

4. Selenite

Selenite can cleanse auras.
https://unsplash.com/photos/vxf-uurQ5rY?utm_source=unsplash&utm_medium=referral&utm_content=creditShareLink

Selenite is an aura-cleansing crystal. When you interact with people throughout your day, the energy around you, commonly known as your aura, can get contaminated with other people's negative and positive energy. So, when your aura darkens, it's time to cleanse it of all the negativity it has acquired. Do you ever feel perpetually exhausted for no reason? This may be your body and mind indicating that your aura needs cleansing. And selenite is the perfect crystal for doing so. It can help rejuvenate the auric field around you, clear out the day's bad energy from your essence, and envelop your body in a peaceful energy flow.

5. Citrine

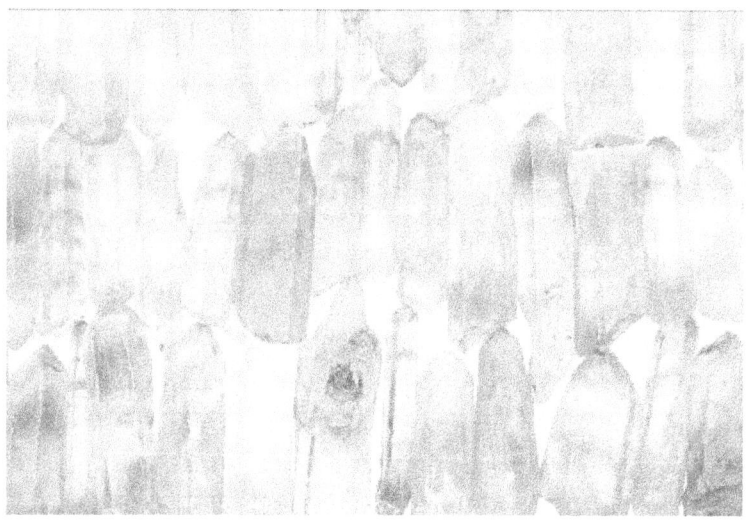

Citrine loosens knotted energy.
https://unsplash.com/photos/ppmiXmhHHyc?utm_source=unsplash&utm_medium=referral&utm_content=creditShareLink

Citrine, a bright yellow quartz crystal, is perfect for use when you're feeling stuck in a situation. This crystal focuses on your solar plexus chakra, which is located near your belly, and helps loosen any knotted energy or tension you have. This crystal can also be used when you're feeling nervous and need an extra confidence boost.

6. Jade

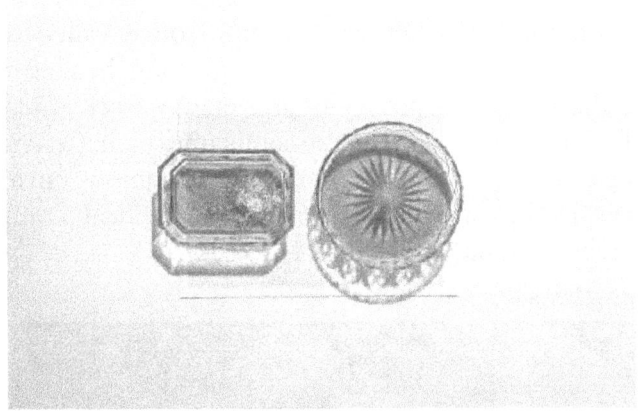

Jade is said to bring fortune.
https://unsplash.com/photos/CrO6G4it4lY?utm_source=unsplash&utm_medium=referral&utm_content=creditShareLink

Jade is the crystal you want if you need a little bit of extra luck in your life. This beautiful green crystal is extremely popular because it is said to bring fortune, abundance, and prosperity in both material and social spheres. Jade jewelry is very common, whether it's necklaces, bracelets, or simple jade rings.

7. Clear Quartz

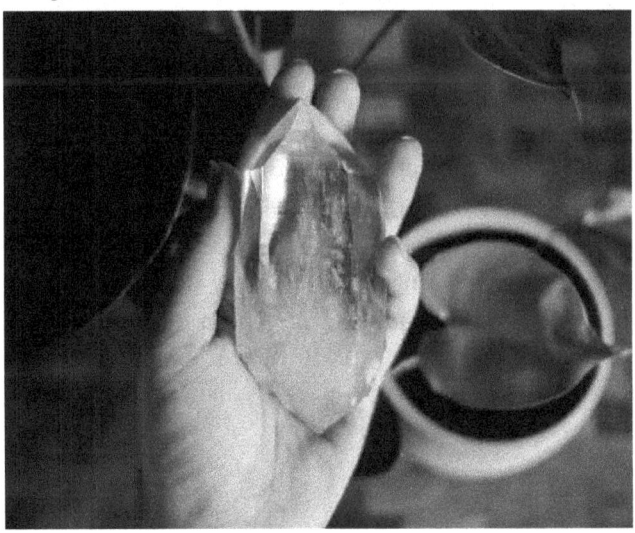

Clear quartz has many healing powers.
https://unsplash.com/photos/IQXhLIoBA8g?utm_source=unsplash&utm_medium=referral&utm_content=creditShareLink

If you plan to have a crystal collection, clear quartz is the first crystal you should get. This crystal is considered essential because of its versatile amplifying properties, which is why it's also often called the "master crystal." This crystal supposedly has numerous healing properties, especially in the realm of spirituality and energy work. Clear quartz is renowned for its ability to cleanse and purify the energetic field, dispelling negative energy and promoting a harmonious environment. It also enhances clarity of thought, making it an ideal companion for meditation, manifestation, and spiritual growth.

8. Rhodochrosite

Rhodochrosite aligns with the heart chakra.
JJ Harrison (https://www.jjharrison.com.au/), CC BY-SA 4.0 <https://creativecommons.org/licenses/by-sa/4.0>, via Wikimedia Commons: https://commons.wikimedia.org/wiki/File:Rhodochrosite_on_Matrix_-_Peru.jpg

Not a very popular crystal but equally beneficial, rhodochrosite is said to help mend a broken heart. Seems like nonsense. This crystal aligns with the heart chakra and carries a gentle yet profound healing energy that can indeed support emotional healing and ease heartache. This crystal is found in varying shades of pink and is usually used as jewelry. This crystal's gentle yet potent vibrations can assist in opening the heart to receive love and joy once more while also encouraging compassion and empathy towards oneself and others.

9. Lapis Lazuli

Lapis lazuli can inspire creativity.
No machine-readable author provided. Adam Ognisty assumed (based on copyright claims)., CC BY 3.0 <https://creativecommons.org/licenses/by/3.0>, via Wikimedia Commons: https://commons.wikimedia.org/wiki/File:1Lapis_lazuli.jpeg

This beautiful blue crystal can hone your creative senses and inspire new and innovative ideas. Whether you're an artist, writer, or engineer, this crystal will help you get your creative wheels turning. This crystal is also known for encouraging clarity and directness, which is especially effective in the workplace. This crystal's energy resonates with the third eye and throat chakras, harmonizing intuition and communication.

10. Chrysocolla

Chrysocolla can aid all chakras.
Rob Lavinsky, iRocks.com – CC-BY-SA-3.0, CC BY-SA 3.0 <https://creativecommons.org/licenses/by-sa/3.0>, via Wikimedia Commons: https://commons.wikimedia.org/wiki/File:Chrysocolla-230109.jpg

This crystal is unlike any other in the sense that it aids all of the chakras instead of just being associated with one. As a result, the chrysocolla gemstone can help your body tune into the latent psychic sensibilities of your soul. Your intuitiveness and spiritual awareness are heightened as the gentle energies of chrysocolla flow through your being. With its vibrant shades of green and blue reminiscent of the Earth and the sea, the chrysocolla radiates a harmonious and soothing energy that resonates with all chakras.

Crystals for Metatron Connection

No doubt crystals hold immense power for healing and spiritual growth, as explored in this chapter. However, the purpose of this chapter was to help you learn how you can use these crystals to connect with the Archangel Metatron. The answer to this lies in the use of specific crystals that are associated with Metatron's qualities. When you use these particular crystals to reach out to him, your intentions will be amplified through these stones and help you establish a profound connection with the Archangel.

1. **Ruby in Fuchsite**

Although a lesser-known crystal, Ruby in Fuchsite holds the captivating energy that resonates with Archangel Metatron. This unique gemstone combines the vibrant red of ruby with the lush green of fuchsite, creating a harmonious union of passion and healing. Ruby in Fuchsite radiates a vibrant energy that ignites the fires of inspiration, creativity, and personal drive. This crystal harmonizes the heart chakra, allowing for the release of emotional blockages and the cultivation of self-love and acceptance. Ruby in Fuchsite also serves as a bridge between the physical and spiritual realms, opening channels for divine guidance and enhancing your connection with the celestial energies of Archangel Metatron.

2. **Fluorite**

This crystal is a kaleidoscope of vibrant colors, ranging from soothing blues and greens to deep purples. This crystal stimulates mental prowess, enhancing concentration and focus, making it an invaluable aid for meditation and deep contemplation. It encourages spiritual growth, helping you navigate the complexities of your spiritual journey with grace and enlightenment. With fluorite as your companion, you can align with the radiant presence of Archangel Metatron, tapping into divine wisdom and experiencing profound spiritual transformation.

3. Unakite

Unakite, a crystal revered by those seeking to connect with the archangel Metatron, holds a profound energy of balance and harmony within it. Combining pink feldspar, green epidote, and clear quartz, unakite emanates a gentle and transformative vibration that aligns with Metatron's guiding presence. This crystal also enhances psychic abilities and intuition, inviting you to explore the realms of higher consciousness and connect with the wisdom of Archangel Metatron.

4. Rainbow Tourmaline

One of the main crystals associated with the archangel Metatron, the rainbow tourmaline, represents the strength, protection, and growth that the angel provides. This crystal is a must-have if you plan to go through a spiritual journey to connect with Metatron, as it will protect your mind, body, and spirit. You can also use it while meditating by simply cupping it in your palms or placing it close to you since it will calm your mind and allow messages from Metatron to be heard.

5. Moss Agate

This crystal contains pure energy associated with nature and the earth. When you go through a spiritual journey, you must stay grounded during the process so you don't get lost or dissociate. Moss agate has a unique healing energy you can manifest during a meditative session to enhance the quality of your spiritual journey and assist in communicating better with the Archangel Metatron.

6. Garnet

Garnet is another crystal favored by the Archangel Metatron and is, therefore, perfect for any spiritual journey you embark on. It is a powerful stone that empowers you to overcome any kind of situation in life. Like Metatron, this crystal can inspire you to overcome even the toughest battles and live your life with love, drive, and passion. Whether facing personal struggles or seeking to manifest your dreams, Garnet's energy aligns with Metatron's divine essence, offering unwavering support and inspiration.

Crystal Cleansing

Keeping a crystal collection can seem pretty simple at first, but there are other considerations you must make once you have these crystals and plan on using them for spiritual connections. As you already know, crystals carry energy, and just like your aura, this crystal energy can also get contaminated with negativity and energy gaps. This is where crystal cleansing comes in. Similar to how you need to cleanse your aura when it's contaminated, you should cleanse your crystals regularly to ensure they're effective during your spiritual practices. There are many methods to cleanse crystals, from simply washing them with tap water to leaving them in a salt bath.

You should use running water for softer stones or let them soak in the sun or moonlight. Water is believed to be a good neutralizer of negative energy and can wash away the contaminations in just 5 to 10 minutes. Sunlight cleansing works best for warm-colored crystals, while moonlight cleansing works better for colder crystals. The sun/moonlight bath is also required when your crystal starts to look dull and drab. You can also try to cleanse your crystals with quartz or selenite. As you've learned in this chapter, both quartz and selenite can cleanse and purify auras, and crystals are no exceptions to this. Another method of cleansing is through smudging, which can be done with a sage stick, sandalwood, or palo santo to create smoke. Finally, you can also soak your crystals in a saltwater bath to cleanse their energy but don't forget to rinse them with regular water afterward.

In conclusion, crystals have held quite a significance in numerous cultures and spiritual practices. They have an array of unique qualities and amplification powers that can help you communicate with the Archangel Metatron. However, beyond simply working with these crystals, a more powerful way to enhance their energy is to program the Archangel's energy into these crystals. To do this, you simply need to set an intention. Hold the crystal in your hand, take a few deep breaths, and close your eyes. Ask the Archangel Metatron to provide you with his energy, and visualize a vibrant beam of light descending from the sky. Imagine this light going into the crystal and enveloping you. After programming the crystals, make sure to cleanse and recharge them as described in the chapter.

Chapter 8: Cord Cutting and Shielding

This chapter is about cord-cutting and energetic shielding methods when Metatron is present. Besides being provided with the definition of cord-cutting and shielding and an explanation of their significance for healing and transformative purposes, you'll be introduced to various techniques for eliminating unwanted ties from your energies.

What Is Cord Cutting?

Cord cutting involves cutting out negative energy from your life.
https://unsplash.com/photos/7NGU2YqBue8?utm_source=unsplash&utm_medium=referral&utm_content=creditShareLink

Throughout your life, you form ties to energies of different levels. Unlike the cords that tie you to high-frequency vibration with uplifting effects, the cords to lower energies have the opposite effect. They generate negative emotions like guilt, fear, pain, and endless worry. Some of these cords can be attached to your loved ones. Yet instead of filling you with happiness and positivity, they're draining your energy, causing it to vibrate at a lower frequency, which isn't conducive to spiritual growth. This happens because you don't have any boundaries in place. However, because these ties are already attached, you need to sever them before establishing healthy boundaries. This is where the practice of cord-cutting comes in.

Cord cutting is the process of releasing unwanted energies from your mind, body, and soul. It also involves self-cleansing and healing from the negative influences of these unwanted attachments or the wounds caused by their release. Many hesitate to go through the cord-cutting process because they think it will harm their relationships. However, this doesn't have to be the case at all. If the relationship is based on mutual trust and love, releasing the unnecessary burdens will only make it stronger. And it's even more critical to sever cords of unhealthy relationships, places, situations, and items. It can do wonders for those struggling to leave behind addiction or other forms of unhealthy behavior.

Whenever you have a negative thought or feeling about something or someone, you send out a cord to its energy. The more often these thoughts and emotions emerge, the thicker the thread gets. Also, the more frequently you send energies through this cord, the more absorbed you will be in its energy and the harder it will be for you to raise your vibrations. This is why it's recommended to cut the cords regularly. It can prevent low vibrations from taking away your joy and the ability to raise your vibrations and experience spiritual growth.

It's equally critical to shield yourself after you've severed the unwanted cords. This way, you can remain free of them longer, and new ties won't attach to you as easily. Establishing a powerful energetic shield will help you defend yourself from negative influence and experience life without unwanted ties attached to you. You won't have to worry about anything or anyone depleting your energy reserves or lowering your vibrations for a very long time. Calling on Metatron for the cutting and shielding process will increase our chances of successfully severing unwanted ties, raising your vibrations, and establishing a favorable energetic flow. And the more you practice this, the more befits you'll see from it, prompting you to keep up the good work.

A Short Cord Cutting Exercise with Archangel Metatron

While many angels can help you with cord-cutting, the process will only be fully successful if you use your own power to eliminate unwanted influences from your life. And who better to call on when you're trying to raise your energies for this task than Metatron, the Archangel of spiritual transformation and ascension? He is always there waiting for you to ask for his assistance on your spiritual journey. However, he lets you walk your path to fully empower you until you call on him. This is his way of teaching you to explore what you need for spiritual growth. The following exercise will help you tap into Metatron's angelic essence and find empowerment for cord-cutting,

Instructions:
1. Light a candle in the name of Metatron, and sit or stand comfortably. Close your eyes, take a few deep breaths, and call on Archangel Metatron:

   "Please, Archangel Metatron, join my side,
   And help cut all the unwanted cords connected to me."

2. Continue breathing in and out and focus on what's happening in and around you. You might feel a tingling sensation in your body, hear a whooshing sound, or suddenly feel lighter.
3. It's also possible that you won't feel anything at all. This is normal, too, so don't feel obligated to expect a specific outcome or feeling. If you do, this might hold you back in the cord-cutting process. Just embrace any sensations or the lack thereof.
4. Have faith in Metatron's power to guide you through the process. Know whether you sense anything or not, it's working because the Archangel is there to assist you. Perhaps you'll start to feel the effects a few days later. If not, you can always repeat the exercise.
5. You may not feel an immediate effect. It might take days or weeks, but you will definitely start to feel a difference in your energy levels.
6. When you practice this exercise regularly, it will become easier, and the results will come faster. With enough practice, you'll feel healthier and lighter – like a weight has been lifted off your

shoulders immediately after the session.

Cord Cutting and Shielding Meditation

Sometimes when you try to cut cords with people, situations, places, or items you strongly connect with, their negative influences will simply re-attach themselves. Even if you channel Archangel Metatron's power to cut unwanted ties, they will return if you don't take measures to shield yourself. This is because you did not address the original issue with the cords. The easiest way to pick up unwanted ties is to be vulnerable due to past hurts. This exercise will help you identify any unwanted cords in your energy field and address why they bring down your energies. As your attention shifts to whatever energy lurking around you that doesn't belong there, you learn why it's critical to healing the underlying issue. You'll also understand how doing it will help prevent them from ever hurting you again.

Instructions:

1. Find a comfortable position and take a few breaths to settle your body and mind. Then recite the following prayer:

    "Archangel Metatron, I ask from my heart and soul for you to join me now,

    So, your love, light, and healing empower me as I cut the cords.

    The ties that bind me to low energies and take me away from spiritual well-being.

    Thank you for hearing my call and supporting me on this task.

    I am now ready to cut the cords and heal the issues they caused.

    Archangel Metatron, I give full permission from my subconscious and conscious mind,

    The depths of my soul and every cell in my body is willing to follow you.

    I am willing to follow your guidance in cutting cords that bind me.

    I invite all the other Archangels, angels, and spiritual guides who wish to join me.

    To assists in this process of cutting cords."

2. It's possible that, despite your declaration, you're still resistant to continuing the process. This is normal, especially if it's your first

time doing this. It's not easy to let go of ties you've held onto for so long. However, letting go of all the resistance is crucial for successful cord-cutting. So, the next step is to channel your energy into this intention.

3. To do this, imagine replacing the resistance with light and self-love. You have the tools for this within you. You just have to reaffirm your power to release the resistance. The following affirmation can help with this:

 "With the power of the spirits and angels that join me,

 I release everything that's preventing me from cutting cords.

 I now declare that I know who I am.

 I know my power and my subconscious mind is open to the divine light.

 Now I complete the process of cutting cords, and it will be done forever."

4. Now, you're ready to call your guides closer. Start by invoking Archangel Metatron, asking him to use his power to assist you in cutting the unwanted ties around you. You may wish to say something like:

 "Archangel Metatron, I ask you to step closer and by my side.

 May I be surrounded by your loving energy and angelic power.

 I ask you to intercede if I struggle to complete the process,

 And empower me as I start cutting the cords that bind me."

5. Visualize the Archangel's light uniting with your energy. Suddenly you can see the unwanted ties that no longer serve you. See the light from within you push the cords away, severing them one by one.

6. Next, call for your own power to heal yourself. Visualize your energy by tapping into your higher self and allowing it to transcend your body, seeping outside and enveloping you in a protective shield. This will be useful when transmuting the cords once Metatron has helped you cut the cords around you. You can reach into your higher self and its energies by saying the following:

 "I ask my higher self to manifest with its bright flames and with all its light.

I ask you to help my conscious self-transmute the cords that I cut,

So, I can heal from their influence."

7. Call on the divine power of the Creator and ask it to empower your healing. Imagine being surrounded by a bright light that shines like a diamond. You will now be prepared for any wounds caused by the unwanted ties to be separated from your energy body.
8. To reinforce your power of keeping the cords away in the future, tap into a mantra that cultivates positive emotions within you. Whatever you say, do it with conviction and in the *present tense*, like you've already accomplished something. For example, you can say:

    "I am now free of unwanted ties."

    "I am now safe from negative influences."

    "Low vibrations can no longer affect me."
9. After reciting your mantra(s), contemplate your newfound empowerment for as long as you feel necessary.
10. Now it's time to express your gratitude for the divine empowerment and Archangel Metatron's assistance in helping you cut the cords and establishing a shield that will dispel them in the future. You can do this by saying the following words of gratitude:

    "Thank you, Archangel Metatron,

    And all the other beings that helped me cut the cords,

    Heal from their influences and keep them away from me in the future.

    I am forever thankful for all these blessings."
11. When you're ready, slowly return to the present. Rejoice in your newfound freedom.
12. If you wish, you can even give yourself a treat for accomplishing this enormous spiritual goal. There is no better way to propel yourself forward in your ascension journey than to do something you enjoy just after you've eliminated the ties that precluded you from enjoying life to the fullest. For example, you can take a walk in nature, write about your experience in your journal or do

whatever your soul desires.

Deep Cord-Cutting Meditation

The following meditation is designed to clear unwanted energetic attachments in your body. It helps eliminate links you have with other people, places, situations, or beliefs. By implementing this cord-cutting exercise into your spiritual practice, you'll clear your subconscious and learn how to call back your power to obtain spiritual freedom. You'll also learn that you don't need to attach yourself to outside energy sources because your biggest source of empowerment comes from within. As you do the exercise, you might feel unexpected emotions bubble up – this is perfectly normal. As you release the cords, remember to be kind to yourself and let the meditation unfold naturally.

Instructions:

1. Settle into a comfortable meditation posture – you can sit cross-legged, lie down, or do whatever feels best for you when doing this exercise. If you choose to lie down, place your hands next to your body, palms up, with the backs of your hands resting on the ground.
2. Take a little time to adjust your posture until you find the perfect place of comfort and ease. If you feel comfortable with it, close your eyes. Deepen your breathing.
3. Feel the cool air entering your body through your nostrils into your lungs. As you exhale, let your whole body soften and relax.
4. On your next inhale, follow your breath as it travels inward and observe whatever sensations are present within you at this moment. Pay attention to the emotions you feel, and let them express themselves fully.
5. Find your way back to that quiet place within you, where nothing can disturb you. Recognize this place as a place of refuge, the spot that's always there, no matter how challenging your life is currently in your outer world.
6. Settle as deeply as you can into this inner stillness. Call upon spiritual improvement by reaching out to Archangel Metatron. Ask him to join you on your cord-cutting journey.
7. Visualize a door that leads to a new environment. Let this door appear fully in your mind's eye – notice its shape, size, and

material.

8. Focus on the door handle; see yourself reaching for it and opening the door. Step through the door and close it behind you. Take in the environment that awaits you. It appears to be nighttime, but the landscape before you is illuminated by the bright silvery light of the full moon.

9. Suddenly, Archangel Metatron appears beside you but doesn't interact with you yet. He knows this is your space, and he lets you explore it. Take a moment to observe your environment, allowing every detail to become more vivid and real.

10. The air is warm, and you can feel the sweet fragrance of flowers that bloom at night. In front of you is a still pool of water. Reflected in it is the light of a thousand stars.

11. Walk toward the pool of water, and sit by its edge. You can feel the pull of water and sense its healing qualities.

12. Move your attention to the natural rhythm of your breath. Notice the small pause between your inhale and exhale. With each inhale, imagine drawing in the silvery light of the moon.

13. Allow the light to fill your inner world as it swirls through your entire body. Suddenly you become aware of a bubble of energy around you. This is your energy body. Use your imagination to tune into this subtle energy layer and sense its cocooning you.

14. Now, switch your awareness to the places in your energy body where unhealthy cords might be attached. Sense these cords however they want to appear. For example, they might come across as ropes, branches, vines, or pipes. Sometimes you will feel where these cords are connected to you – you might sense them as hooks, arrows, plugs, anchors, or any connection types. Other times you will not.

15. Approach the cords with curiosity and without judgment. Tap into these energetic attachments and pay attention to whatever you notice in them. If you have trouble identifying or reaching into the cords, ask Metatron to help you.

16. Take a deep breath to yourself, and repeat the following:

    "With Archangel Metatron by my side,

    I reclaim my own energy.

    I release these cords and attachments."

17. Deepen your breath and fill yourself up with even more light. Feel how the light slowly pushes out the unwanted attachments as they start disconnecting from your energy body. You might feel hot or cold, or strong sensations rise up.
18. Continue breathing deeply until all the attachments are removed from your energy body. If you wish, you can imagine yourself reaching for one of the disconnected cords and taking it into your hands.
19. Dip the cord into the healing water in front of you, sealing the connection. Pull on the cord until it stretches and let go, sending it back to where it came from. To ensure you'll be shielded from it in the future, say:

    "Thank you, I release you."
20. Repeat the step above with all the cords you wish to permanently eliminate from your life. When you reach the last one, take a deep breath, exhale, and dip your toes into the water.
21. Feel the warmth of the water nourish your body and slowly lower yourself into it. You feel loved and supported. If you wish, imagine yourself staying back and admiring the blanket of stars and the bright full moon in the sky.
22. Feel yourself being filled with fresh, new energy to replace the void left after the unwanted energies left your body, mind, and soul. As you emerge from the water, you see that your energy body is now clear of any blemishes.
23. Look at Archangel Metatron and soak in his healing and empowering energies, allowing your mind to become still.
24. Feel the shift in your body and mind, and commit to becoming unapologetic with your boundaries in the future. Promise yourself that you'll release and dispel any unhealthy energies should you come in contact with them to protect your precious energy.
25. Thank the energies and Metatron for the blessing of being free of unwanted cords and feeling that you're powerful. When you feel it's time to leave, look for the door you came in through.
26. Walk through the door, close it behind you, and slowly bring yourself back to the present. Feel the hardness of the surface beneath you and let it bring you back fully.

27. With slow movements and perhaps a sigh, come back to your space by opening your eyes. Be prepared for any energetic influences that might want to reach out to you. It's common for energies to want to attach themselves back to you. However, if you're prepared for them, they won't be able to do you any harm.

Chapter 9: Daily Meditations

The Archangel Metatron has left many doors open for us to connect with him and ask for his guidance. While there are numerous other ways to communicate with the Archangel of inspiration and creativity, meditations take the number one spot when hoping to strengthen your bond with Metatron or ask him for guidance. Meditation is a powerful way to connect with your higher consciousness and reach out to celestial beings for their divine guidance. They help you relax and be mindful of the present moment while also enjoying the peace and tranquility that comes with a true inner connection with the Archangel Metatron. All you have to do is connect through your open heart and ask for help.

Using meditation and tools, you can spiritually develop with Metatron.
https://unsplash.com/photos/x5hyhMBjR3M?utm_source=unsplash&utm_medium=referral&utm_content=creditShareLink

Not only are meditative rituals great when asking for help with spiritual development and learning, but also when you need to cleanse your energy and gain inspiration, insight, or confidence about a particular situation in your life. Guided meditation is indeed a very powerful tool for spiritual enlightenment, and angels, specifically archangels, play a major role in meditative sessions. In fact, Metatron is considered to be the master of higher self-meditations and is the best Archangel to call upon when you're meditating for spiritual guidance. When you connect with a celestial being like Metatron, you'll see an improvement in your spirituality as a whole and a difference in your meditating experiences.

While you've gone through the pillar of light meditative sequences, there's still much to uncover regarding Metatron-related meditation practices and rituals. So, this chapter will act as your guide to some daily meditations you can perform to gain spiritual wisdom from none other than the archangel of wisdom. In this chapter, you'll go through several types of meditation practices combined with Metatron's invocation. Whether you want to cleanse your energy with the help of Metatron's light or become aware and mindful through an awareness meditation ritual, this chapter has it all.

Energy Cleansing Meditation

As you've learned throughout the previous chapters, everything in this world consists of energy, whether material objects or living beings. Imagine how many people you meet throughout your day, not just people; you come in contact with different environments and situations where you absorb and exchange energy. This is where your energy can get contaminated and stagnant, negatively affecting your well-being. For instance, have you ever had a day where you were around a fight or some other negative situation and just felt anxious or fatigued for no reason? Maybe the fight wasn't even connected to you, but you still feel as if the negativity of the situation rubbed off on you. Well, this isn't just a feeling, but what happens, which is why cleaning your energy and restoring balance is crucial.

This is where energy-cleansing meditation comes in. You've already learned about other tools that can help with aura cleansing, but there's nothing better than a smooth session of cleansing meditation with Metatron's energy and blessings. The Archangel serves as an invaluable guide through the meditative process, and using his profound wisdom, he can help reach your chakras and provide additional support during the process. Metatron can be called upon before starting the meditative process to adjust your ascension frequency and align your chakras. This will result in the elimination of any energy blockages and imbalances you may have.

Preparation:
1. Before you can invoke the blessings of Archangel Metatron, it's essential to create a suitable meditation space with candles and incense if needed. You can also add the crystals favored by Metatron to aid the process.
2. Next, you need to ground and center yourself on the earth chakra star, which is present beneath your feet.
3. Then, designate the created space for meditation by invoking an ascension column of light, platinum net, and ascension flame from the Archangel Metatron. Ask him to provide the space with high-frequency energy and provide protection.
4. Also, request Metatron to place a golden dome of protection around your meditation space to keep it clear of any negative energies.

Setting Intentions:
5. Now, it's time to sit comfortably in the space you've created and close your eyes. Take a deep breath and visualize yourself journeying to the Archangel Metatron's temple through your higher consciousness.
6. Visualize the temple radiating deep shades of pink and dark green, constructed with sacred geometric shapes. As you approach, imagine the temple doors automatically opening for you.
7. In the center of the temple, visualize Metatron awaiting you with his arms stretched in front of him, and between his arms, the delicate and intricate Metatron's cube is rotating. Let your gaze focus on the cube.
8. Ask the angel to remove all negative energies from your life, and imagine these negative energies as black balls. Envision these balls being sucked from your aura and toward the cube.

Breathwork and Visualization

9. While imagining all the negative energy leaving your aura, your breathing should be slow and stable. Inhale deeply for five seconds, then hold for five and exhale for five seconds to form a rhythmic breathing pattern.
10. Visualize Metatron's cube absorbing all the negativity from your life. Feel the cube spin clockwise while destroying the balls of negative energy.
11. Allow the spinning cube to further expel any excess dark energy from your body and aura. As the negative energy is expelled, you'll start to feel lighter.

Body Scan

12. Do a slow body scan from head to toe to feel any areas of tension, heaviness, or discomfort that might remain.
13. If you still feel any tightness or tension in your body, visualize the cube's cleansing energy moving toward those areas and washing away any impurities.

Grounding and Integration

14. Once you're done with the visualization process, take a few moments to ground yourself and feel the cleansing experience.
15. Express gratitude to Archangel Metatron for his support and guidance.
16. Slowly start returning to your regular state of awareness, moving back from your higher consciousness.
17. Stretch your hands and feet, and feel your body making contact with the ground.
18. Finally, open your eyes, and blow out the candles to conclude the meditative session.

Breath Awareness Meditation

Breath awareness meditation can be done for various reasons, including reducing stress, regulating emotions, improving mindfulness, and enhancing spiritual insight. When done with the invocation of the Archangel Metatron, this meditative technique is also known as Merkaba heart meditation. The process involves certain visualizations that get the body, mind, and spirit in tune with lower and higher vibrations, spinning them into an energy vehicle at the heart center. This technique involves mindful meditation coupled with breathing exercises that align the heart chakra with Metatron's energies and help fill up your body with love.

Preparation
1. Start with finding a quiet, comfortable space where you won't be disturbed.
2. Cleanse the space of any negative energy by smudging or crystal cleansing.
3. Take a relaxed position on the ground or a yoga mat, dim the lights, and close your eyes.
4. Take a moment to invoke the presence of the Archangel Metatron and ask him for guidance and clarity through the meditative session.

Focusing on the Breath

5. Bring your attention to the sensation of your breath as you inhale and exhale slowly.
6. Focus on the natural pattern of your breath without trying to control it.
7. Observe the rise and fall of your abdomen and feel the sensation of your breath passing through your nostrils.

Cultivating Awareness

8. While you're focusing on your breathing, you'll likely get distracted by thoughts, emotions, or sensations. When you do, you should observe them without judgment and bring your focus back to your breathing.
9. Whenever your mind wanders, make sure you bring your attention back to your breath, making it an anchor for your focus.
10. Whatever arises during your awareness session, keep a calm and curious attitude toward it without thinking about it excessively.

Deepening the Practice

11. To deepen the practice, start by placing your hands on top of your chest. Your left hand should be placed first, followed by your right.
12. Exhale deeply, and visualize a brilliant ball of light or energy moving from your heart to all parts of your body until it engulfs you completely.
13. Visualize this loving heart energy flowing into your left hand, moving through the entire left side and into the right side of your body.
14. Allow this light to get brighter and stronger while moving through your body, flowing in a figure-eight pattern (through all eight chakras)
15. As you breathe in, envision yourself in the space between the center of the earth and the sun, with the sun shining its bright light right above you.
16. Then, imagine a beam of loving power shooting from the start of the universe to the end, passing through the center of the galaxy, the center of the earth, and connecting with the center of every atom in the world.
17. Imagine yourself floating, with the sun above your head aligned with your spine and the heart chakra, while the lower energies of the earth should be aligned below your spine.
18. Experience the higher energies of the sun moving into your body as you're drawn upwards. Imagine the light passing through your crown, flowing into your head, face, spinal cord, and every system of your body from top to bottom. At the same time, feel yourself being drawn downwards toward the lower, calm, and cool energies of the earth. This will create a balance of energy, with your body floating in between these two visualizations.

Closing and Integration

19. Feel the love energy flowing through your body as you exhale, and allow this energy to expand naturally until it engulfs your whole body.

20. Envision your body getting larger with the light, expanding until it becomes the size of the whole planet, the solar system, the galaxy, and the whole universe.
21. Feel yourself become one with the universe and realize the vast energy within you. Be mindful of every sensation you're feeling.
22. Continue breathing and visualizing this energy as long as you want while also envisioning Metatron's cube spinning within your heart.
23. With each exhale, breathe out pure love and radiate it to every part of your body, extending it to the universe.

Akashic Records Meditation (Advanced)

Akashic records meditation with Metatron's guidance is the perfect option for people who want to take their meditation game to the next level. This meditation technique is for advanced spiritual practitioners who want to access their Akashic Records and gain more spiritual wisdom to reach a higher state of consciousness. Think of the Akashic Records as a warehouse of information or a cosmic computer that contains all the records of your life. These records contain every feeling, intention, and situation you've had. These records are said to be stored in the etheric plane, and they also contain psychic information about a person's lifetime of experiences. To read and understand the Akashic Records, a person has to rise above their physical form and gain a non-linear, higher-dimensional awareness.

Akashic Records are also sometimes known as the "Book of Life." It holds the vibrational records of everything and everyone that has existed in this universe. These records contain the very lifetimes of all the souls to have existed. The vibrational body of these records is located in the etheric region, everywhere, at all times. These records are continually updated as the world goes on and contain future points of choice and possibilities. As you take a breath, get a thought, set an intention, and make a move, these records keep being updated with your every move, every choice, and every thought. So, how do these records relate to the Archangel Metatron? The powerful Archangel is responsible for encoding and recording everything in the Akashic Records.

Consequently, only Archangel Metatron can help you access these records and improve your spiritual self. Of course, this doesn't mean you'll be able to read about future events or change your future, but you will be able to align your past skills and resources while also healing the present blockages tied to your past. The best way to access these records is through a deep meditative session guided by none other than the Archangel Metatron himself.

Preparation

1. Prepare a suitable meditation space where you'll be away from noise and won't be disturbed.
2. Dim the lights, and light some candles near you. Place a few crystals around your meditation space, like rainbow tourmaline or garnet.
3. Close your eyes, and invoke the presence of the Archangel Metatron. Call upon him, and ask him to surround your space with divine white light.

Visualization and Protection

4. Visualize the angel enlightening your space with brilliant white light, and take a few deep breaths.
5. Imagine you're sitting in this beautiful light and exhale as you let go of any stress, tension, or pain you're feeling.
6. Breathe the pure energy in, and along with it, absorb the positive vibes, love, strength, and relaxation
7. Ask the Archangel to let you access the divine Akashic Records to gain wisdom, knowledge, and clarity.
8. Now, envision a ball of pure energy as big as you; this is where the Akashic records are held. To enter within, you'll need to lift your vibration and achieve a very pure light frequency.
9. Once you've reached the higher consciousness, ask Metatron to guide you into the dimensional understanding of the Akashic Records.

Deepening the Meditative State

10. Now, it's time to deepen the meditative state and visualize deeper. Imagine an elevator of light appears as soon as you enter the ball of light.
11. Visualize yourself stepping into this elevator, and feel the doors close behind you. As the elevator moves upward, feel yourself

moving closer to the divine.

12. Open up your heart and tune into the infinite connections of the divine flowing through you. Feel your mind expanding with the energy flowing all around you. Imagine this energy entering your heart until you feel love, light, and joy wash over you.
13. Once the elevator opens up, step out into the sacred space, and take a deep breath to submerse yourself in the conscious realm of the Akashic Records.
14. For a few moments, take some deep breaths and remain mindful of the present moment. Calmly observe the knowledge encoded in the white light surrounding you. Try to examine the records present in this energy, and notice how every soul is interlaced with each other. Realize the interconnectedness between all things and how individual choices can cause a ripple far and wide.
15. Take a moment to observe your connection to the records, to the universe, and to all that exists.

Exploring the Akashic Records

16. To explore the Akashic records, consider a situation or question you need guidance for or answered. Archangel Metatron will be there to guide you toward the right answer.
17. Ask your question out loud, and let the answer appear in the space in front of you, like being in a magical library. You may envision that Metatron is handing you a book, a scroll, a simple piece of paper, or even a visual where you can explore your life and get the insight you need.
18. Just trust your intuition and the Archangel's guiding hand, and you'll find the solution to your problem.
19. Keep in mind that the Archangel is assisting you; open your heart to the Akash emerging before you, and receive the guidance you need.

Closing and Integration

20. Once you've gotten your answers, or have had a revelation, express your immense gratitude to the Archangel and the Akashic Records. Imagine you're stepping away from the scene

and back into the elevator of light.
21. The elevator will gracefully and swiftly take you back, after which you should take a deep breath, lower your frequencies and step out of the glowing white ball of energy.
22. Slowly return your awareness to your physical body. In the next instant, take a moment to write down or record the guidance and answers you received from your spiritual journey. Write every little detail down, including your feelings, impressions, insights, and any unknown symbols or knowledge you've received.
23. Don't wait to note down this information because it can escape your mind soon, similar to how a dream drifts away after you wake up.
24. Although you may not fully understand what you've gained during this session, once you write it down and contemplate it, you're more likely to make sense of the whole thing.

You can gain a wealth of information and knowledge about your soul and psychic consciousness through the dedicated practice of guided meditative sessions from Metatron. As you continue on this journey, don't lose patience with yourself, everyone's journey looks a little different and can take considerable time. You should allow yourself enough time to attune to the frequency of Metatron and hope for the best. Although various forms of meditation serve as effective pathways to connect with Archangel Metatron, the key to a successful session lies in maintaining unwavering faith and belief in the guiding light of Metatron. *Trust that he will provide the necessary assistance and guidance in navigating the challenges you may be facing.*

Bonus: Correspondences Sheet

This chapter provides an easy-to-check reference of all correspondences associated with Archangel Metatron. Feel free to use them when you want to connect or work with this Archangel.

Festivals or Feasts of the Year

Metatron can be celebrated any day or part of the year – although he is the most powerful on Friday night and Saturday morning. In some parts of the world, a festival celebrating Archangel Metatron is held on September 29, the international day of the Archangels.

Colors Associated with Metatron

The typical colors attributed to Metatron are white, black, and rainbow. White symbolizes his angelic purity and his place in the angelic hierarchy. Black is a complementary color to white, indicating Metatron's ability to establish harmony and balance between different aspects of life. The rainbow color alludes to Metatron's colorful aura and is often depicted on the Metatron cube.

Zodiac Signs and Planets

Archangel Metatron is linked to all the zodiac signs because he rules all months and planets. However, he has a particularly strong link to Virgo. He helps this sign establish their path in life and allows this sign to explore their limitations and set boundaries, preventing them from venturing too far away. He might also help Virgos banish low-vibrating energies and motivate them to become more productive - especially when it comes to utilizing the divine blessing they receive.

Angel Numbers

Angel numbers are numeral symbols sent by the angels, communicating their messages. Regularly seeing specific numbers could represent that a particular angel is nearby and wants to talk to you. Metatron, for example, often communicates through the number 11. Most of the time, this number will appear in duplicate. For example, you might see 11:11 on your clock mid-morning, and the same number appears again on a receipt. If it appears several times in a row as a synchronicity, it might be a sign that Metatron is calling you. He often sends this message when trying to bring one's attention to finding life's purpose or a connection you need to make for spiritual growth. He might use it to guide you on your path to ascension or signal that you're ready to awaken your spirituality and elevate it to a higher level.

Symbols and Sigil

Cord

Metatron is often depicted severing ties - a symbol of his ability to guide people through cord-cutting. With the Archangel's help, you can release yourself from unwanted connections and heal from their effects while raising your vibrations.

Brightly Colored Lights

Bright swirls of a colorful aura and colorful lights are often linked to Metatron - with purple and red being the most prevailing colors. Metatron's aura combines his connection to the heavenly realm (manifesting in violet spiritual energy) and his link to the earthly realm (appearing as a red light). Besides these, Metatron's aura might also contain rays of bright pink, white, and dark green.

Crown Chakra

Those working with Metatron often experience a tingling sensation that begins at the crown of the head. This is where the crown chakra is located and where you can receive the most support from Metatron. The crown chakra is the gateway for high-frequency energies you can call on during experiences like the pillar of light meditation and others.

Metatron can help activate this chakra and remove any blockage.

The Solar Plexus Chakra

Besides the crown chakra, Archangel Metatron is also associated with the third, or solar, plexus chakra. Because this energy point is linked to personal power, self-mastery, and sense of self, working with Metatron can help you enhance all these qualities.

Buzzing Noises

If you're sensitive to auditory signals, Metatron often communicates through a high-frequency buzzing noise in your left ear. Besides indicating the Archangel's proximity, this sign is also one of his favorite ways of sending direct messages. Some say that if you listen closely, you can hear his faint voice telling you how to move forward with your goals and life.

Overpowering Scents

Those more sensitive to olfactory signals often associate Archangel Metatron with overpowering aromas that appear out of nowhere. For example, if you're walking on the street and suddenly encounter a floral fragrance with no flowers or people wearing perfumes nearby, this could be a sign of Metatron trying to reach out to you.

Diamond White Light

One of the most common ways Metatron sends his messages is through flashes of white light that shine bright like a diamond. This Archangel's essence is so powerful that it's meant to be a shining light that brings inspiration and motivates your spiritual growth.

The Pillar of Light

Metatron is often visualized as providing empowerment by standing close to a pillar or column of light. Some say that this column appears as a fire that burns with flames so bright it can blind a person if they look at it directly.

The Metatron Cube

The Metatron cube is a symbol associated with sacred geometry. It depicts 13 spheres, which are arranged to form two hexagrams. This unique shape is said to exemplify every power in the universe – from the smallest to the all-consuming ones. It also depicts the energy that connects all things. Because of this symbolism, the Metatron cube is often used as an energetic conductor by those who wish to harness positive energies and banish negative vibes. For the same reason, this object vibrates at very high levels – and can serve as a powerful protection against low-vibrating energies.

The Tree of Life

Archangel Metatron is portrayed as the guardian of the Kabbalistic Tree of Life, presiding on its crown (also known as Kether). In art, Metatron's connection is seen in the images that paint him as a magnificent creature wearing a multicolored robe with several pairs of golden wings. The golden color of the wings is linked to the high aspect of the crown. The robe's different colors (pink, blue, green) speak of Metatron's all-encompassing power as the ruler of the Tree of Life.

Book of Life

Also known as the Akashic Record, the Book of Life is a collection of records of peoples' and angels' actions, indicating who is eligible for spiritual elevation and granted entrance to heaven and who isn't. As the divine scribe, Metatron is often depicted recording good acts in the Book of Life in art.

Metatron's Sigil

Metatron's sigil is a special symbol associated with this Archangel. It's represented by a single letter that combines two letters. It generally resembles the letter "A," except one leg of this letter is formed by the letter "M," which is located on the lower end of this leg and is turned upside down. The sigil is often used to invoke Metatron's guidance, protection, and healing during spiritual work.

Trees, Plants, Herbs, and Oils

Metatron is usually linked to lavender and jasmine, which can be used to attract self-love and obtain tranquility, happiness, beauty, wealth, and luck. Using geranium rose and lime when working with Metatron can improve your health, strengthen your connection to loved ones, and protect yourself from bad luck, misfortune, injuries, and illnesses.

Other trees, herbs, and plants associated with Metatron include almonds, mistletoe, orchids, dill, ylang-ylang, basil, chrysanthemums, wild rose, white rose, lilies, and carnations.

Essential oils to use when working with Metatron are frankincense, benzoin, sandalwood, roman chamomile, myrrh, cedar, vetiver, cypress, patchouli, rose, neroli, juniper, geranium, tangerine, jasmine, and lavender. All these are known for facilitating spiritual elevation and can serve as reminders of the benefits of abandoning materialistic thoughts for a peaceful transition of one's soul.

Crystals and Metals

Diamonds, white crystals, and other stones of empowerment. For the best effects, use a clear crystal to connect the energies of other stones and unite them in high-frequency vibrational energy. Clear quartz is one of the most powerful crystals in the spiritual world. You can imbue it with any intention and use the crystal's vibrations to amplify your intention and manifest it.

Labradorite is another crustal you can use when working with Metatron. It's a stone with incredible protective abilities that can help you block intrusive energies. It's useful for recalling hurtful memories if you want to heal your energy and your ties with your loved ones. You can also benefit from using labradorite when communicating with Metatron to decipher any signals you receive in dreamwork or while journeying.

As their name implies, meteorite metals have a powerful connection to the universe. This also links them to one of the most powerful angelic beings who distributes energies and records happenings in this universe. These metals are often used to represent Metatron in rituals and ceremonies – whether in the piece of metal object that holds other tools or as the main element used for the Metatron cube.

General Associations

Spiritual and Religious Intentions

Metatron can teach you how to enhance your magical abilities and, if necessary, find a magic teacher or coven you can learn from. He empowers people's religious nature, often helping them find enlightenment through religion or discover their life path and gain spiritual knowledge within a religious community. He can also help you uncover and understand karmic paths in life.

Metatron is responsible for being an angelic energy source, the being that gives you "the wings" you need to overcome obstacles, the guide for transcending pain and healing from traumas, the angel that manipulates spiritual paths, the second greatest source of divine power, the lord of the afterlife and heaven, the incarnation of a fully ascended human, a cosmic guardian, the manipulator of the portals between realms. He is also responsible for providing divine assistance, establishing divine authority, banishing negative energies, facilitating reincarnation, empowering with a supreme voice, preventing evil influences from entering heaven, the ultimate power to release unwanted ties, awareness of multidimensionality, granting psychic abilities like teleportation, telekinesis, knowledge projection, spiritual healing, granting immortality to souls.

Metatron is further linked to spell casting and supports those who venture into angelic magic or want to explore resurrection, gain increased strength and stamina for spiritual work, endure hardships for growth, and renew their spirits repeatedly until they reach ascension.

As the divine scribe, Metatron possesses a great deal of cosmic knowledge. He can even erase warnings and remove negative protective sigils and give you strategies for dispelling negativity from one's life.

Metatron is keen on supporting those who work toward goals that benefit everyone around them. He awakens powers, virtues, values, and talents that help people to persevere on this path. He cleanses the body, mind, and spirit, restoring balance and contributing to overall well-being. Working with Metatron sharpens your mind, opens you up to new ideas and visions, and helps you tap into your intuition and sense spiritual communication. He can also help you see your reality more clearly and other people's views without judgment and accept it so you can get along with others.

Qualities he can help you cherish: spiritual growth, connection to the light body, seeking divine union, energetic activation, and ascension.

Due to having firsthand knowledge of the records contained in the Book of Life, Metatron knows how negative thoughts can lead to disproportionate actions and undesirable outcomes. Because of this, he will always encourage people to embrace positive thought processes. He knows these lead to better choices and outcomes – and you can only gain from positive thinking.

Indigo and Crystal Children

While Metatron is the patron of all children who struggle to thrive, he is particularly protective of so-called crystal and indigo children. These children are highly sensitive to energetic shifts and more open to spiritual communication. However, these children are prone to pick up negativity because of their innate connection to the spiritual realm and energies around them. It permeates their energetic bodies, depleting them of their energy and causing emotional, mental, physical, and spiritual imbalances. On a positive note, these children are more likely to pick up clues from spiritual guides early in life. For example, Metatron might appear to them as he feels they need his help to become their best version. Metatron can help them tear down antiquated beliefs and build communities that serve the greater good. He teaches them skills of empowerment and gives them tools such as fearless courage, enabling them to fulfill their life's purposes.

Tarot Cards

The Judgment

The first Tarot card associated with Archangel Metatron is the Judgement. It's a symbol of rising vibrations and embracing a higher level of consciousness – and it's easy to see why it's linked to this angel. If this card comes up, it might indicate that Metatron is suggesting that you're starting your spiritual awakening. Heed his call and act on it by tuning into his higher frequency so you can step into the newer version of yourself.

This card can also carry a message urging you to make a potentially life-altering decision. To make this decision, you must combine your intellect and intuition. If you're at a crossroads, Metatron might be signaling that any choice you make now will have long-lasting effects. He tells you that before making a decision, tap into your higher self and trust whatever you see there.

The Judgment card can also pop up when you're close to a significant stage in your spiritual journey. Perhaps it's time to review and evaluate your past experiences and learn from them. Now that all pieces of the puzzle of your life are finally coming together, it's more important than ever to make a conscious decision. Only this will allow you to heal your wounds and put the past behind you. You will let go of regrets and release any sadness or guilt about past events.

The Fool

The Fool is a card denoting new beginnings, having faith in the future, being inexperienced, not knowing what to expect, having beginner's luck, improvisation, and believing in the universe as the Fool stands at the beginning of his journey and is about to venture into the unknown. On his journey, the Fool will receive guidance from much-treasured sources. Similarly, Archangel Metatron is the treasure holder of angelic wisdom, which he uses to guide souls through life, death, and beyond. This card might indicate that although you might not know where you're going yet, you shouldn't worry because Metatron will be there to guide your spirit.

The card could also be a reminder to keep an open, curious mind and see everything as an exciting opportunity instead of a challenge. Leap into new experiences, and you will soon have personal growth and spiritual development. Experiment with different forms of spiritual work and do your best to learn about your spiritual allies, including Metatron. It will help you connect to his energy and all the other energies around you. Tap into this energy and uncover your fullest potential by letting your heart, mind, and soul be free of burdens and negativity.

The Chariot

The third Tarot card attributed to Archangel Metatron is the Chariot – the symbol of willpower, achievements, self-discipline, and public recognition. If Metatron is sending you this card, it means he saw that you'd overcome a challenging situation and managed to keep your energies in balance. He was glad to observe that you took the time to view the situation from different angles and make a decision based on this. It means you've gained his approval, and he encourages you to enjoy your accomplishment and keep up the good work. If you're yet to overcome a situation, Metatron is signaling you to remain grounded so you can think clearly about what you want to achieve. Maintaining self-control will make it easier to keep up the determination to do whatever it takes to succeed. At the same time, Metatron is cautioning you to be kind to others. Feel free to use this card as a motivation to boost your energy levels to stay true to your priorities. Combining this card with the Metatron cube in spiritual work is believed to help harness the Archangel's ability to warp time and shorten the timeframe you need to manifest your dreams.

The Dreamer

In Angelic Tarot, Metatron is associated with the Dreamer. This card signifies your entrance into a new and exciting stage of life. Metatron might send you this card to tell you that you should believe in yourself, indicating you should have faith in your ability to succeed and take the steps you need to move forward. He might also signal that you should listen to your intuition and be open about the guidance you receive from spiritual sources. As the angel of spiritual transformation, Archangel Metatron will always gladly oversee those embarking on their first spiritual journey. If he sends you the dreamer card, take a leap of faith and follow his signals. It takes strength, courage, confidence, and believing in yourself. It can even be scary, but in the end, it's an exhilarating prospect that activates spiritual growth and ascension. The card might also be Metatron's way of telling you to use faith and courage to combat negative energies of fear and doubt. Put your faith in his divine guidance, and you won't regret it. You'll gain a powerful ally in Metatron and all the knowledge you need to empower your inner guidance and connection to the divine essence.

Other Correspondences

- **Month:** All months
- **The day of the week:** Friday and Saturday
- **The hour of the day:** The hours between sunset on Friday and sunrise on Saturday
- **Season:** Fall
- **Deities:** Ceres, Demeter, Thoth
- **Body parts ruled:** Skeletal system, the spine, stomach, legs, and skin
- **Animals and mythical creatures**: Horse
- **Direction:** Center
- **Element:** Earth

Conclusion

Whether you're a beginner at Angelic Magic or have some experience in the topic and are interested in alternative ways to heal spiritual traumas to become empowered, hopefully, this book gave you enough information to heal, empower and transform yourself. This book sets out something for everyone, from easy-to-do exercises to more advanced spiritual teachings. And most importantly, you had the chance to explore the spiritual, cultural, and religious background of Archangel Metatron, – along with a review of the basic spiritual concepts associated with him.

Those who needed a stepping stone for further exploration of personal ascension had a chapter dedicated to explaining the process and its importance, together with exercises to facilitate this process. In the subsequent chapter, you've learned about the signs Metatron might send you after you've initiated the first contact seeking healing, protection, or guidance to ascend. Meanwhile, those looking to expand their knowledge got to delve deeper into the ascension process by exploring some of the most powerful spiritual tools associated with Metatron.

One of the first spiritual instruments you've learned about was the Metatron cube, a symbol based on sacred geometry often used for energy transfer. As one of the most influential Archangels, Metatron's energy vibrates at incredibly high frequencies. Implementing the Metatron Cube into your practices can help you connect with his energy, regardless of your vibrational levels. As an angel, Metatron is also associated with light (often used to symbolize his power in visualization exercises), so another great tool to connect with him is the Pillar of Light Meditation.

Due to his immense energy and willingness to share it with those seeking spiritual healing, Archangel Metatron is the perfect ally for energetic healing methods like Reiki. Angelic Reiki is one of the most popular ways of self-healing – and for a good reason. It empowers your energy body to eliminate unwanted disturbances. Crystals vibrating at high frequencies have the same effect because they carry unique healing powers. Moreover, they can be imbued with the intention of healing or banishing negativity, as well as connecting with Metatron, who will further empower you on whatever journey you decide to take.

Those who had trouble eliminating negativity from their lives or experiencing the return of negative influence despite banishing them have likely found the chapter about cord-cutting most helpful. Besides explaining the importance of cutting unwanted ties, the chapter also offered practices for creating an energetic shield that will prevent the unhealthy cords from re-attaching you again. As you've learned, when this exercise is performed in the presence of Metatron, it will have a long-lasting effect. It will also help you heal from the influences of low-energy cords and their sudden release from your energetic body.

Archangel Metatron can be a powerful ally in any spiritual journey. Whatever your goal is for reaching out to him, know that he will always be there to assist you. However, to make the most out of your connection with this angel, you must nurture it – and the best way to do it is through daily practices. Even spending a few minutes a day will work wonders on your spiritual development. And if you have trouble incorporating the celebration of Metatron into your day-to-day schedule, you only need to revisit the correspondence sheet at the end of the book to find the tools to best represent him.

Here's another book by Mari Silva that you might like

Your Free Gift
(only available for a limited time)

Thanks for getting this book! If you want to learn more about various spirituality topics, then join Mari Silva's community and get a free guided meditation MP3 for awakening your third eye. This guided meditation mp3 is designed to open and strengthen ones third eye so you can experience a higher state of consciousness. Simply visit the link below the image to get started.

https://spiritualityspot.com/meditation

References

A beginner's guide to 10 types of crystals & how to use each of them. (2021, May 12). Mindbodygreen. https://www.mindbodygreen.com/articles/types-of-crystals

Adele, T. (2023, April 6). Healing crystals: Benefits, uses, and where to buy. Forbes. https://www.forbes.com/health/mind/guide-to-healing-crystals/

Ali, Herman, L., Believe, S., & Wille. (2021, January 15). Archangel Metatron: 7 Ways to Recognize and Connect with Him. A Little Spark of Joy. https://www.alittlesparkofjoy.com/archangel-metatron/

Angelic reiki healing. (n.d.). Naturallygiven.com. https://naturallygiven.com/angelic-reiki-healing-session/

Angelic Reiki. (2021, February 25). Christine Ringrose. https://www.christineringrose.co.uk/treatments/angelic-reiki/

Apollo, A. (2015, November 12). Activate your Pillar of Light. Guardian Alliance. https://guardianalliance.academy/healer/activate-your-pillar-of-light/

Aquarius. Academy ~ 𝓜 ~ School of Consciousness. (2018, April 21). Metatron's Cube Heart Meditation. Lightwork. https://medium.com/working-light/metatrons-cube-heart-meditation-5936e241464d

Archangel & Zodiac Signs. (2020, March 3). AstroTalk Blog – Online Astrology Consultation with Astrologer. https://astrotalk.com/astrology-blog/archangel-and-zodiac-signs/

Archangel Metatron Meditation. (2018, February 12). Padre. https://www.guardian-angel-reading.com/blog-of-the-angels/archangel-metatron-meditation/

Archangel Metatron, The Arcahnegl of the Planet Earth – Traditional Magical Correspondences. (n.d.). Archangels-and-Angels.Com. http://www.archangels-and-angels.com/aa_pages/correspondences/angel_planet/archangel_metatron.html

Archangel Metatron. (n.d.). Circleofangels.Nl. https://circleofangels.nl/?page_id=2199

Archangel Metatron: Everything You Need To Know About Him. (2022, October 10). My Today's Horoscope. https://mytodayshoroscope.com/who-is-the-metatron-angel/

Archangel Metatron: Heal your energy. (n.d.). Jennroyster.com. https://www.jennroyster.com/blog/archangel-metatron-heal-your-energy

Archangel Metatron: The Mighty Angel of Judaism. (2021, November 26). OshaeIfa.com. https://en.oshaeifa.com/angelology/archangel-metatron/

Archangel Metatron's cube healing & activation. (2022, August 26). Vince Gowmon. https://www.vincegowmon.com/archangel-metatrons-cube-healing-activation/

Beckler, M. (2011, August 27). New Archangel Metatron meditation. Ask-angels.com. https://www.ask-angels.com/free-angel-messages/new-archangel-metatron-meditation/

Bedosky, L., & Laube, J. (n.d.). Reiki: How this energy healing works and its health benefits. Everydayhealth.com. https://www.everydayhealth.com/reiki/

Bellino, G. Z. (n.d.). From Enoch to metatron. Shulcloud.Com. https://images.shulcloud.com/609/uploads/class_files/Pardes/04aFromEnochtoMetatronSOURCES.pdf

Brown, S. (2019, May 17). Who is Archangel Metatron? And What is The Metatron Cube? The Black Feather Intuitive. https://www.theblackfeatherintuitive.com/archangel-metatron/

Brown, S. (2019, May 17). Who is Archangel Metatron? And What is The Metatron Cube? The Black Feather Intuitive. https://www.theblackfeatherintuitive.com/archangel-metatron/

Brown, S. (2019, May 17). Who is Archangel Metatron? And What is The Metatron Cube? The Black Feather Intuitive. https://www.theblackfeatherintuitive.com/archangel-metatron/

Conscious Vibe. (2022, March 4). Fascinating origin of Metatron's Cube: Meaning & symbolism. The Conscious Vibe. https://theconsciousvibe.com/the-symbolic-meaning-behind-metatrons-cube-sacred-geometry-explained/

CosmicSurfer. (2011, December 17). Michael vs. Metatron (biblical versions). SpaceBattles. https://forums.spacebattles.com/threads/michael-vs-metatron-biblical-versions.210468/

Crawford, H. (2019, December 15). Are you guided by archangel Metatron? Here's compelling 9 signs that you are.... Numerologist.com. https://numerologist.com/spiritual-growth/spiritual-world/9-signs-guided-by-archangel-metatron/

Crystals and archangels: Series intro. (n.d.). Healingcrystals.com. https://www.healingcrystals.com/Crystals_and_Archangels__Series_Intro_Articles_1789.html

Crystals for spiritual healing. (2022, January 20). Moonrise Crystals. https://moonrisecrystals.com/crystals-spiritual-healing/

Desy, P. L. (2015, January 25). 5 traditional Usui reiki symbols and their meanings. Learn Religions. https://www.learnreligions.com/usui-reiki-symbols-1731682

Discover the folklore of gemstone magic and crystal healing. (2021, December 28). The Creative Cottage. https://thecreativecottage.net/healing-properties-of-gemstones/

Dublin, A. (2023, April 26). Metatron: the most Powerful Angel in the Celestial Hierarchy. The Grimoires Corner. https://www.thegrimoirescorner.com/2023/04/metatron-most-powerful-angel-in.html

Enlightenment, V. A. P. (2017, June 26). 7 The Chariot - Archangel Metatron - Angel Tarot Cards. DREAM WEAVER. https://enlightment1.wordpress.com/2017/06/26/7-the-chariot-archangel-metatron-angel-tarot-cards/

Get guidance from archangel Metatron and the number 11. (n.d.). Pandagossips.com. https://pandagossips.com/posts/6442

Heart, A. L. (n.d.). Archangel Metatron -. Angel Light Heart Blog. https://angeltherapycoach.wordpress.com/tag/archangel-metatron/

Hopler, W. (2012, April 18). How to recognize archangel metatron. Learn Religions. https://www.learnreligions.com/how-to-recognize-archangel-metatron-124277

Hopler, W. (2013, January 1). Archangel Metatron's cube in sacred geometry. Learn Religions. https://www.learnreligions.com/archangel-metatrons-cube-in-sacred-geometry-124293

Hopler, W. (n.d.). How to Recognize Archangel Metatron. Learn Religions. https://www.learnreligions.com/how-to-recognize-archangel-metatron-124277

Hughes, D. (2022, May 4). What is angelic reiki? Divine Escape. https://www.divineescape.co.uk/post/what-is-angelic-reiki

Insight Network, Inc. (n.d.). Daily Multidimensional Clearing With Archangel Metatron. Insighttimer.Com. https://insighttimer.com/kristintaylorintuitive/guided-meditations/multidimensional-general-clearing-meditation-and-connection-to-archangel-metatron-life-upgrade-psychic-clearing-and-protection-cutting-cords-highest-good-activation

Insight Network, Inc. (n.d.). Divine Alignment With Archangel Metatron. Insighttimer.Com. https://insighttimer.com/kristintaylorintuitive/guided-meditations/divine-alignment-with-archangel-metatron-life-upgrade-energy-clearing-psychic-clearing-and-protection-deep-spiritual-cleansing

Insight Network, Inc. (n.d.). Pillar Of Light. Insighttimer.Com. https://insighttimer.com/awakenedlife/guided-meditations/pillar-of-light-meditation

Judgement Tarot Card Meanings. (2011, December 22). Biddy Tarot. https://www.biddytarot.com/tarot-card-meanings/major-arcana/judgement/

Lazzerini, E. (2022, February 10). Archangel crystals & angel healing stones revealed. Ethan Lazzerini. https://www.ethanlazzerini.com/archangel-crystals/

Lewis, B. (2022, November 15). The meaning of Metatron's cube: Definition and origin - GFL. Galactic Federation Of Light. https://www.galacticfederationoflight.com/blogs/consciousness/what-is-meaning-metatrons-cube-sacred-geometry

Linda. (2020, April 3). Pillar of Light Meditation. Thought Change. https://thoughtchange.com/pausing-to-discover-yourself/

lucifall. (2010, August 21). The Fool and Temperance and The High Priestess and The Pargod. Tarot Forum. https://www.tarotforum.net/threads/the-fool-and-temperance-and-the-high-priestess-and-the-pargod.145106/

Maggie. (2022, November 25). Metatron: Make an altar to the archangel of understanding. Spiru. https://spiru.com/metatron-make-an-altar-to-the-archangel-of-understanding/

Maloney, J. (2022, June 15). Personal and Planetary Ascension. Spirituality+Health. https://www.spiritualityhealth.com/personal-and-planetary-ascension

Manolo. (2022, October 14). Archangel Metatron: Everything You Need To Know. Better Numerology. https://www.betternumerology.com/archangel-metatron-everything-you-need-to-know/

Manolo. (2022a, January 1). Archangel Colors: The 7 divine rays of light. Better Numerology. https://www.betternumerology.com/archangel-colors/

Manolo. (2022b, October 14). Archangel Metatron: Everything you need to know. Better Numerology. https://www.betternumerology.com/archangel-metatron-everything-you-need-to-know/

Marshall, L. (2022, October 23). Reiki symbols: Meaning and drawings of each. Drawings Of. https://drawingsof.com/reiki-symbols/

Metatron Significance & Facts. (n.d.). Study.Com. https://study.com/academy/lesson/metatron-significance-facts-archangel.html

Metatron. (2015, December 23). ZAYAT AROMA. https://www.zayataroma.com/en/oils/metatron

Metatron. (n.d.). Angelology Wiki. https://angelology.fandom.com/wiki/Metatron

Metatron's cube: What it means in sacred geometry. (2023, March 15). WikiHow. https://www.wikihow.com/Metatron%27s-Cube

myspiritualshenanigans. (2020, May 30). 10 Stages Of Spiritual Awakening & Tips To Master Spiritual Growth. My Spiritual Shenanigans. https://myspiritualshenanigans.blog/stages-of-a-spiritual-awakening/

Newman, T. (2017, September 6). Reiki: What is it, and are there benefits? Medicalnewstoday.com. https://www.medicalnewstoday.com/articles/308772

Oracle, D. ~. A. (2013, August 7). Archangel Metatron ~ The Dreamer. Archangel Oracle. https://archangeloracle.com/2013/08/07/archangel-metatron-the-dreamer/

Rand, W. (2006, March 1). Knowing which Reiki techniques to use. Reiki. https://www.reiki.org/articles/knowing-which-reiki-techniques-use

Reddit - dive into anything. (n.d.). Reddit.com. https://www.reddit.com/r/Soulnexus/comments/gctn3b/my_amazing_meditation_experience_with_archangel/

Reiki symbols & their meanings: Everything you need to know. (2018, May 8). Mindbodygreen. https://www.mindbodygreen.com/articles/reiki-symbols-meanings

Roots, A. (n.d.). Connecting with Archangels. Angelic Roots. https://www.angelicroots.com/products/connecting-with-archangels-archangel-metatron-rainbow-tourmaline-moss-agate-and-garnet

Salow, S. (2022, May 18). How to Activate Your Pillar of Light & Why It's Essential. SYLVIA SALOW. https://sylviasalow.com/2022/05/18/activate-your-pillar-of-light/

Sievert, M. (n.d.). No title. Joynumber.com. https://joynumber.com/archangel-metatron/

Sinclair, G. (2019, December 18). 11 signs you're being guided by archangel metatron. Awareness Act. https://awarenessact.com/11-signs-youre-being-guided-by-archangel-metatron/

Spiritual. (2015, November 27). Angel Hierarchy - The Three Spheres Of Heaven. Spiritual Experience.

Stardust, L. (2020, December 22). The 10 most common types of crystals—and what they're used for. Oprah Daily. https://www.oprahdaily.com/life/a35045011/types-of-crystals/

Stewart, T. (2021, September 5). How to use crystals & stones for spirituality (ultimate beginner guide). Whimsy Soul. https://whimsysoul.com/how-to-use-crystals-stones-for-spirituality-ultimate-beginner-guide/

Support, W. W. a. (2020, March 30). How to Cut Cords with the Angels. Caroline Palmy. https://carolinepalmy.com/how-to-cut-cords-with-the-angels/

The benefits of crystal therapy – and why we think it rocks! (2016, May 4). Devonshire Dome. https://www.devonshiredome.co.uk/news/the-benefits-of-crystal-therapy-and-why-we-think-it-rocks/

The Fool Tarot Card Meanings. (2011, December 23). Biddy Tarot. https://www.biddytarot.com/tarot-card-meanings/major-arcana/fool/

The Ultimate 10 Step Guide To Cutting Cords Forever. (2020, June 26). Georgie G Deyn. https://www.georgiegdeyn.com/ultimate-10-step-guide-to-cutting-cords-forever/

victoriaGB. (2022, November 3). Cord Cutting Meditation. Gabbybernstein.Com. https://gabbybernstein.com/cut-the-cord/

Who is Archangel Metatron? The angel of the Akashic Records, Soul Ascension and 5D – Angel Readings, Angel Healings, Psychic Medium. (2022, March 18). Angel Readings, Angel Healings, Psychic Medium. https://archangelwisdom.com/who-is-archangel-metatron/

Wille. (2021, January 15). Archangel metatron: 7 ways to recognize and connect with him. A Little Spark of Joy. https://www.alittlesparkofjoy.com/archangel-metatron/

Zhelyazkov, Y. (2023, March 13). What is Metatron's cube symbol and why is it significant? Symbol Sage. https://symbolsage.com/metatron-cube-symbolism

www.ingramcontent.com/pod-product-compliance
Lightning Source LLC
Chambersburg PA
CBHW051848160426
43209CB00006B/1213